DIGITIZING YOUR COLLECTION

DIGITIZING YOUR COLLECTION

PUBLIC LIBRARY SUCCESS STORIES

◄ **SUSANNE CARO** ►

WITH CONTRIBUTIONS BY SAM MEISTER, TAMMY RAVAS, AND WENDY WALKER

edition

An imprint of the American

Chicago 2016

ISBNs
978-0-8389-1383-3 (paper)
978-0-8389-1400-7 (PDF)
978-0-8389-1401-4 (ePub)
978-0-8389-1402-1 (Kindle)

Library of Congress Cataloging-in-Publication Data [to come]

Names: Caro, Susanne, 1980- author. | Meister, Sam, author. | Ravas, Tammy, 1977- author. | Walker, Wendy, 1974- author.
Title: Digitizing your collection : public library success stories / Susanne Caro ; with contributions by Sam Meister, Tammy Ravas, and Wendy Walker.
Description: Chicago : ALA Editions, an imprint of the American Library Association, 2016. | Includes bibliographical references and index.
Identifiers: LCCN 2015032866 | ISBN 9780838913833 (print : alk. paper)
Subjects: LCSH: Library materials—Digitization. | Library materials—Conservation and restoration. | Libraries—Special collections—Electronic information resources. | Digital preservation. | Public libraries—United States—Case studies.
Classification: LCC Z701.3.D54 C37 2016 | DDC 025.8/4—dc23 LC record available at http://lccn.loc.gov/2015032866

Book design by Alejandra Diaz in the Calluna and Brandon Grotesque typefaces.
Cover images courtesy of the Library of Congress.

♾ This paper meets the requirements of ANSI/NISO Z39.48-1992 (Permanence of Paper).

Printed in the United States of America
20 19 18 17 16   5 4 3 2 1

CONTENTS

Acknowledgments   vii
Introduction: Why Digitize?   ix

1 WHAT TO CONSIDER BEFORE DIGITIZING 1

2 DIGITIZING COPYRIGHTED MATERIALS 25

3 OVERCOMING STAFFING LIMITATIONS 51

4 GETTING YOUR COMMUNITY INVOLVED 75

5 FUNDING OPPORTUNITIES 97

6 MARKETING YOUR COLLECTION 117

7 DIGITAL PRESERVATION 133

Resources   147
About the Author and Contributors   151
Index   153

ACKNOWLEDGMENTS

T he state librarian had declared we would have a digitization project and the task fell to me. I had no experience and had to develop the project from the ground up. My search for papers and other documentation provided best practices but no examples of how libraries like mine managed with little budget and few staff. That project, and a desire to collect stories of how libraries manage to place great resources online led to this book. During this project I learned the importance of having support both inside and outside of my library. I owe a great deal of thanks to Monica Villaire-Garcia who mastered the metadata and Laurie Canepa, my supervisor who provided so much support, and Shelley Thompson and Cynthia Baughman of *El Palacio* magazine, who were eager to have 100 years of their magazine online.

As the idea of collecting these stories was developed I asked three of my talented colleagues to lend their expertise. Professor Wendy Walker had experience with creating a digital collection in Nevada. She provided insights, interviewed several librarians, and provided considerable editing assistance. Digital Preservationist Sam Meister is well versed in how to maintain and care for digital files, and this knowledge is reflected in his chapter on "Digital Preservation." Tammy Ravas wrote the chapter on "Digitizing Copyrighted Materials."

I would also like to thank the many librarians around the country who were willing to answer my many questions and share their stories.

INTRODUCTION
WHY DIGITIZE?

We are that public library ideal of a people's university and the way we are connecting
with our public is changing, but I think the goals of that connection are no different.

—Eileen O'Connell, branch manager, Special Collections Library,
Albuquerque/Bernalillo County Library, New Mexico

L ibrary patrons continue to expect more online content, and libraries
are attempting to meet these expectations with article databases and
e-book collections. According to a 2011 survey by the Institute of
Museum and Library Services (IMLS), libraries had 35 million e-books
available.[1] Why should libraries invest additional time and funds to
scan old paper documents, add metadata and store them in an accessible electronic collection when they are already providing access to databases? As your
community accesses your collection online and uses more electronic content
your collections can be hidden if they are not accessible online. Through
digitization you can increase access and awareness of your unique collections,
from fragile photographs to microfilm. The electronic versions act as surrogates,
reducing handling of the originals, and can be used to preserve your valuable,
tangible materials.

EXPECTATIONS OF YOUR COMMUNITY

As digital technology becomes more ubiquitous in daily life it can be easy
to forget that it was not always there. On library discussion lists such as
Publibs, librarians often share head-scratching requests: people looking for
film of Lincoln's assassination, photographs of George Washington or Jesus.[2]
Technologies such as photography and film have existed for so long that
people can forget that they have not always existed. Don't be surprised when
a patron asks for a digital copy of a World War II document with the expectation that it should have been originally created in an electronic format.

These types of interactions will only increase over time. The Mindset List, published by Beloit College each year, provides insights into the experiences that have shaped incoming college freshmen. The class of 2015 has always had Internet access. The class of 2016 has always lived in cyberspace and prefers digital cameras, and the class of 2017 has always had access to the Global Positioning System (GPS). Soon there will be college freshmen who have always had access to e-books.

As more people are born into a world where most information is created digitally, the expectation for all library collections to be available electronically will continue to grow and users will expect that content to be available in a variety of formats and on multiple devices. The number of people with Internet access in the United States has increased significantly over the last ten years. In 2013 the U.S. Census estimated that 83.8 percent of households had a computer, and 73.4 percent had Internet access. In 2013 the Federal Communications Commission reported 86 million residential fixed-location Internet connections and 142 million mobile wireless service subscribers.[3] More people are now able to access your library's holdings from home or on a mobile device. Responding to the public's interest in digital content, libraries have increased the number of databases in their collections. Libraries are meeting the growing demand for electronic materials with historic newspaper databases, genealogy resources, and e-books.[4]

The desire to access materials online is part of a trend in libraries toward digital inclusion and providing a range of digital content and access options. Digital inclusion is described as having three to four aspects. A Pew Research Study looked at access, adoption, and application while the Digital Inclusion survey considered public access, digital content, digital literacy, and domain-specific services and programs.[5] According to the 2013 Digital Inclusion Survey, 100 percent of libraries offer public Internet access, 98 percent offer some form of technology training, and 62 percent report that they are the only source of free Internet access in their community.[6] Public libraries strive to meet the technology needs of their users, and as more people become accustomed to accessing e-books and online articles they will expect to find other library materials online as well. It is a good strategy to engage users by including digital versions of a library's unique holdings in addition to the latest best sellers or magazines.

DIGITIZING TO IMPROVE ACCESS

Digital access redefines a library community from geographically-based to interest-based. Individuals who no longer live in their hometown are able to access digital versions of their high school yearbooks. People who have never lived near your library can find your collections online and even volunteer or donate relevant materials. Researchers, historians, and school children from all around the world will be able to find and use your library's digitized collections. Users are already looking for information from their local and state governments. A Pew survey found that 35 percent of Internet users have used the Internet to research official government documents or statistics.[7] Town reports, vital statistics, planning documents, committee minutes, and more can be made available through the library's digital collections.

Online access can increase interest in your collections and the use of the tangible materials by increasing discovery and awareness of your holdings. According to librarian Julie Warren, images from the collection at Georgetown County Library have been used by *ABC Nightly News* and PBS for news programs and *Antiques Roadshow*. Library users value the ability to access digital collections and consider digitization to be an important service. Madison Library in New Hampshire surveyed the town to learn how the community ranked library services, including their digitization efforts. According to former director Mary Cronin, the results revealed that 78 percent of people felt it was important or very important for the library to continue to add to its digital collections. Online collections allow libraries to reach users outside of the physical library building and to meet user expectations for digital resources. Once a collection is online it is set free; it is available around the world at any time.

DIGITIZATION AS A PRESERVATION TOOL

Preservation of original materials is another reason to digitize. Over time scrapbooks, photographs, audio, video, and other items can start to degrade. In some cases (consider deteriorating audiocassettes) digitization can prevent a total loss of content. For items such as photographs, digitization and subsequent digital restoration can help you make high-quality items available to your users without altering the original material. Some materials are more likely to be damaged by repeated physical use, such as brittle newspapers or yearbooks that have had photographs removed by former students. Digitization allows the materials to be used without the wear and tear of handling.

If you are digitizing purely for access, ask yourself what will happen if you lose your file. Will you be willing to re-create all the work? Will you still have access to the originals and will they be in a condition suitable for rescanning? Even if you are not considering using digitization to ensure continued access to material, you should consider best practices to protect the investment of time and money that goes into creating a digital collection. If you are concerned about keeping your collection available for future generations, there are resources which can guide your process.

Synopsis

The three main reasons why you should digitize are:

- **Expectation:** As more information becomes available electronically, your users will expect your unique collections to be available digitally.
- **Access:** Making your collections available online increases access within and outside of your community.
- **Preservation:** Some media like newspapers, photographs, and cassette tapes are already in a state of deterioration. Digitization can help preserve the content of these media for the future.

NOTES

1. Deanne W. Swan et al., *Public Libraries in the United States Survey: Fiscal Year 2011* (Washington, DC: Institute of Museum and Library Services, 2014), 8, www.imls .gov/assets/1/workflow_staging/AssetManager/4487.PDF.www.imls.gov/assets/1/ workflow_staging/AssetManager/4487.PDF.
2. Robert Balliot, "Library One-Liners," in *The Best of Publib* (blog), April 27, 2013, https://bestofpublib.wordpress.com/2013/05/26/library-one-liners.
3. Federal Communications Commission, *Internet Access Services: Status as of June 30, 2013: Industry Analysis and Technology Division Wireline Competition Bureau. Federal Communications Commission, June 2014* (Washington, DC), www.fcc.gov/ document/fcc-releases-new-data-internet-access-services-1.
4. Katherine Zickuhr, Lee Rainie, and Kristen Purcell, "Library Services in the Digital Age," Pew Research Center, January 22, 2013, http://libraries.pewinternet .org/2013/01/22/library-services/.
5. "What Is Digital Inclusion?" Digital Inclusion Survey, http://digitalinclusion.umd .edu/content/what-digital-inclusion. John Carlo Bertot et al., "2013 Digital Inclusion Survey: Survey Findings and Results Executive Summary," Information Policy & Access Center, July 21, 2014, http://digitalinclusion.umd.edu/sites/default/files/ uploads/2013DigitalInclusionExecutiveSummary.pdf.
6. Bertot et al., "2013 Digital Inclusion Survey."
7. Aaron Smith, "Government Online: The Internet Gives Citizens New Paths to Government Services and Information," Pew Internet & American Life Project, April 27, 2010, www.pewinternet.org/files/old-media//Files/Reports/2010/PIP _Government_Online_2010_with_topline.pdf.

CHAPTER 1

WHAT TO CONSIDER BEFORE DIGITIZING

What is truly ours that's unique and what do we have an obligation to preserve?

—Frank Somers, Adult Services Librarian, Bethlehem Public Library, New York

Something wonderful may be stored behind a locked door, in a filing cabinet, or in a basement at your institution. You know more people would like to be able to access this material but due to their condition or other issues it is only made available to patrons on request and cotton gloves may be required to handle the item. These materials could be a scrapbook with the photos falling out from use by generations of students or a bound newspaper that may crumble with one more turn of the page. It could be a series of handwritten letters or a collection of photographs that are completely unique to your library. Selecting the material to be digitized may be one of the simplest parts of the digitization process. Every library potentially has something that it wishes to share more broadly but for various reasons cannot. Digitization allows more patrons to see photographs from your collections, or a local history pamphlet, without the risk of damage or loss.

Every step of your digitization process will be determined by the collection. An important question to consider is whether or not the material is too rare to leave the library. There are some materials you may not be willing to trust with the postal service or strangers at a company providing digitization services. It may be a Civil War diary, rare glass-plate photographic negatives, or a painting by a local artist. The item may be too large to safely ship, such as oversized atlases or even furniture. If you are afraid to let an item leave the library you will need to consider the equipment and staff available at your institution.

If your collection is large, such as long runs of newspapers, reports, or rolls of microfilm, outsourcing to a digitization vendor may be an option. Depending on the services offered by a vendor, your library may need to provide descriptive metadata, but scanning and even storage may be handled off-site from your library. Another important question to consider is whether you are willing to trade control of a collection in order to have another entity deal with management of the digital files. If you work with a consortium which hosts the files and provides access, you may not be able to alter metadata yourself. This may be a minor inconvenience when compared to managing the online access or paying for a content management system like CONTENTdm.

WHAT IS THE INTENTION OF THE COLLECTION?

The creation of your digital collection will be guided by the reason behind its development and the intended use. Asking yourself why you want to digitize and what you hope to accomplish are an important part of the pre-digitization process. If you are pulling together materials to celebrate an anniversary, subject, or event, your project may have a fixed date of completion with no intention to add to the collection beyond a certain point. You will not need to consistently find funding to add material on an ongoing basis. If the collection is opened with the intention of growing, regular funding, staff and ongoing equipment purchases need to be considered. Some libraries start with a limited plan but will expand to include more materials. Other libraries may be content to have a finished project.

Other considerations:

- If the intention is to improve access, how will users locate the collection?
- Will there be a link on the library's main page, in catalog records, or included within a subpage such as "local history"?
- What level of metadata will be included to make the materials more searchable, and will text documents have optical character recognition (OCR) allowing searching within the text?
- Do you have a plan to promote the collection before and after it is available?

- Will there be restrictions to access?
- If you are using digitization as a preservation tool, what kinds of digital files will you create and how will you maintain them?
- Does your intended audience require any special or unique presentation, access features, or functionality?
- Based on your intended audiences, what kind and how much metadata will you need to include for searching and discoverability?

CHOOSING THE COLLECTION

One of the most important issues to consider when looking for a collection to digitize is if the material is unique, rare, or of strong local interest. Photographs, postcards, letters, journals, scrapbooks, newspapers, booklets on local history, high school yearbooks, and other materials may only be found in your library. If the materials were created by a member of your community, the chances are good that yours is the only library which has that material.

A collection is not just a stack of papers or a selection of objects, but also a connection to the community and a story waiting to be told. Strong candidates for digitization include materials that focus on something unique to your city or collection. Many libraries are digitizing materials that are important to the community and in doing so show how much the library values local history, stories, and people.

Photographs

If you had to evacuate and knew there was a chance your home would be destroyed, what would you take with you? There are a number of lists compiled by government agencies that include radios, food, medication, and water, but what items are irreplaceable? Many people would include photo albums, and a camera or hard drive with documents and photos. Images are important links to the past, a way to leave one's mark, to document and capture moments fleeting in time. During the creation of a photograph the click of the shutter, the image exposed to film or translated to pixels suggests a level of fidelity. The image is expected to accurately portray the moment and the flaws. Eyes caught in mid-blink and the blur of movement reinforce this sense that the image is true. The interest in the image is enhanced if there is a personal connection. Family photo albums are cherished items, something to be rescued from fires and other disasters as irreplaceable. The value is personal memory caught on paper.

Digital Images Created to Reduce Handling and Improve Access

A popular item or collection can be damaged by repeated use. Making the material available online can increase access while reducing the number of hands on the original materials, which can thus be kept more secure. According to Kathy Robins, library information systems coordinator at Billings Public Library in Montana, her best candidate for a digital project was a collection of photos of the "people who came here with the railroad: merchants and bankers and people who started businesses and ranches." These original images capture the faces of people who came west in hopes of a better life, work, and riches in Montana. Users were required to request these images, which were kept under lock and key, and were then left alone with the photos in the Montana Room. Library staff did not believe they were losing many or any of the images with this arrangement, but they felt that this was not the most secure manner for handling these one-of-a-kind items.

Access to the library's hundreds of images was limited to patrons who were physically present and knew to ask for them. The library felt the collection "should be available online and also by doing that we would be able to preserve them in case they disappear." Once digitized, details in photographs can emerge as the viewer zooms in on faces, clothing, shoes, or other objects. Billings Public Library has made available over 600 photographs in the Montana Memory Project. In one photograph, an enlarged portrait of early resident Henry G. Williams reveals the pattern on his tie. In another, a portrait of Mrs. Williams shows a blouse with pleats, two different types of lace, and an intricate broach studded with seed pearls. The images may be useful for those studying fashion and design, but they also reveal personal details. Fraternity pins often indicate social connections. The clothing or favorite pieces of jewelry likely held meaning for the wearer who chose those articles for a formal portrait. Jennie Appelman, an older woman with a heavily lined face and snow-white hair, sports a small jeweled brooch, a corsage of what may be violets and two strands of very small, narrow conical shells.[1]

The Billings Public Library has helped to preserve the original images by creating digital surrogates. This has improved access by allowing more users to directly access the materials online. This is reflected in the statistic for the collection which shows over 10,000 page views since the collection was made available. Furthermore, now students and researchers can enlarge images to see details and print their own copies.

Preserving Community Memories

Digital copies can help reduce wear and tear on original photographs, but in some cases the digital version is created with the goal of saving an image.

The materials and processes used to create photographic images can lead to a number of preservation issues ranging from cracked glass-plate negatives to the breakdown of binders and emulsions, UV damage, tarnish, and acid damage from scrapbook papers, glue, tape, and humidity. In some cases there may be no way to arrest the deterioration. For libraries that consider themselves to be guardians of the past, digitization is a process that can be used to capture images for preservation purposes and safeguard local history when physical preservation methods no longer suffice.

The Georgetown County Library in South Carolina is in an area vulnerable to hurricanes, and there is a real danger that images and documents could be lost in a natural disaster. The library has a digital collection titled the "Georgetown County Hurricane Collection" documenting the destruction, including the two most destructive storms: Hurricane Hazel in 1954 and Hurricane Hugo in 1989. Flooded streets only recognizable by lines of trees, roofless homes, and beach houses cracked in half are testimony to the sudden violence of storms which have the potential to hit each season. With each storm there is a possibility of lost mementos and history.

The library recognized the preservation potential of digitization when it scanned the Morgan-Trenholm collection of photographs. According to digital librarian Julie Warren, Georgetown Mayor W. D. Morgan hired a photographer to document the community in the early years of the twentieth century and during a large exposition in Charleston. The images of new sidewalks and recently planted trees promoted Georgetown as a modern and attractive community. Images of everyday activities provide a brief glimpse of the lives of regular people. These photographs, once intended to promote a city looking to the future, now document the history of the Georgetown community, allowing users to see what has changed or remained the same over the years.

Looking beyond its own materials, the Georgetown County Library also works with local museums on projects where the community is invited to bring their family photographs to the library to be digitized. The efforts are intended to preserve copies of the images before disaster strikes. Photographs are returned to the owners in archival envelopes. This service creates goodwill in the community by demonstrating that the library values and invests in personal and community history. Julie Warren described one interaction where a regular patron brought some images to the library. Some of these were in scrapbooks, others were loose in a cardboard box. After scanning, these items were returned in archival boxes and the woman was "just thrilled" with the new packaging and the digital copy of her material. Warren considers this service to be mutually beneficial to the library and to the community. Should there be fires or floods those precious images which are stored by OCLC (Online

Computer Library Center) and the library both on- and off-site will still be available to families and friends. The library is considering additional storage locations outside of Georgetown for additional security. Warren jokes that should the community be hit by another hurricane she will have to flee with copies of the files, but the library is serious about keeping backups and doing all it can to protect Georgetown's history.

Collections to Honor and Remember

Photographic images provoke curiosity, stir emotion, and are powerful reminders of the people and events in a community. One collection which shows the daily life of a town, the horrors of war, and the dedication of a local celebrity can be found at Flora Public Library, in a small town with a lot of community pride located 100 miles east of St. Louis, Missouri. When the library felt the need to develop a digital collection, the work of one man was the obvious choice, and the library developed the Charles Overstreet collection.

Overstreet lived in Flora for most of his life. He was a character and, in the 1970s, mayor and a local celebrity after the town garnered national attention with the creation of a rap video in a bid to have a prison constructed there.[2] Overstreet was widely respected in the community, and the librarians knew of his collection, part of which had been compiled into two books titled *Charley's Flora* (2000) and *More Charley's Flora* (2007). The librarians determined his work would be of local interest and of considerable historical value. Images taken during his service in World War II would also be in demand with the approaching anniversary of that war.

Overstreet regularly gave talks about his experiences in the war to school children and was seen at most community functions with his camera. His love of photography may have begun during his service in the war when as a corporal and army photographer he documented his experiences in Europe. His photographs from that time period show the people he served with, the crumbling ruins of bombed-out buildings, and the massacre of prisoners at the German prison camp Gardelegen. Deploying in 1943 with the 252nd Field Artillery Battalion, he left his new bride, Catherine, behind. On October 9, 1944, his unit landed on Omaha Beach in France, and from there he would travel through France, Belgium and finally through Germany with the Ninth Army.[3]

The variety of photos, spanning decades and covering both the war in Europe and life in Flora, meant Overstreet's images would likely be of interest to a wide audience. Dona Cory, director of the Flora Public Library, explained that "it wasn't just a Flora collection, it was something that people everywhere could be interested in." The materials in the Overstreet collection were so far reaching that the librarians felt it would give them a great chance to secure grant funding. The need to digitize the materials was also influenced by the pressure of time. The librarians knew they would need Overstreet's knowledge of the photos' subject matter to create and compile accurate metadata. Perhaps even more importantly, they wanted Overstreet to be able to see his collection online and experience how much the community appreciated his many years spent documenting life in Flora.

The World War II segment of the collection has received international attention. A man in Germany contacted the library after he found a photo of his grandparent's home. A woman from Wisconsin who had accessed the collection online contacted the library after finding a picture of her father who served with Overstreet. Other images are heart-wrenching, such as documentation of the overt horror and inhumanity at Gardelegen. Captured in stark black and white, these may be some of the most accessible images showing the remains of over 1,000 people murdered by Nazis as U.S. troops advanced to the prison camp. Flags were lowered in Flora when Overstreet passed away in 2010. Flora lost Charlie Overstreet, but his collection remains available to the community and to the world. With the anniversary of World War II, and the loss of veterans, these images are of increasing interest and importance.

Current Images and Cultural Expression

At the Nisqually Tribal Library in Olympia, Washington, there is a photograph collection documenting a modern event. The Canoe Journeys started in 1989 with "Paddle to Seattle" and has continued with 60–80 canoe groups participating each year. A local photographer, Allen Frazier, had photographed the journeys for eighteen years and was willing to work with librarian Faith Hagenhofer to determine which images could be digitized and to provide metadata.

The Nisqually Tribal Library was awarded a grant for the collection to be added to the Washington Rural Heritage Project (WRHP), which is managed by the Washington State Library to provide a platform for the collections of small, rural libraries and cultural institutions. Coordination activities, scanning, and metadata entry tasks were all performed by library staff. The description of the collection from the WRHP site states: "The Tribe's pride of place and history are once again enriching the lives of young and old alike. The Nisqually Canoe family has learned and taught many of the older skills, and these practices are once again taken up by community members."[4] The event and collection are important to the community. One of the advantages of making these images available online is that they can be shared with outsiders who cannot attend or may have never heard of the event. The Canoe Journeys are a combination of cultural, social, political, and spiritual practices, and portions of the event are not intended to be shared outside of the community. What images are shared depend on the mindful and respectful curation of the material. Hagenhofer and Frazier selected images that represented the event, but also excluded images intended to be viewed only by tribal members.

According to Hagenhofer, in creating this collection the library has altered its image from one of a place that collects information to one which also actively engages in creating content from a Nisqually perspective. This content reflects and increases awareness of the importance of local events. This was a very intentional decision on the part of the library. The Canoe Journeys were determined to be different from other collections currently available online, and Hagenhofer wanted more than a collection of materials relating "to known historical events. We really wanted to start with something that was locally really important but not necessarily well known." Awareness of the event has grown since the first journey. According to Fawn Sharp, president of the Quinault Nation, the event is seen as "a touchstone gathering for the tribes of the Pacific Northwest—one of the largest traditional gatherings of indigenous people anywhere in the world."[5] Now, thanks to the efforts of the Nisqually Tribal Library and the generosity of Allen Frazier, the world can see the canoes and people involved in this wonderful celebration.

Yearbooks

You open the book and see rows of smiling faces. Hair, glasses, and clothing give a quick clue about the age of the photographs. You are looking at a high school yearbook, a record of students, fashion, and a time capsule for a single year. Yearbooks are great local records that are often found only in schools, public libraries, and the collections of former students. They are excellent examples of unique, high-interest items found in many public libraries.

Yearbooks are often some of the most popular items in a library, especially among alumni and genealogists. When Geoff Kirkpatrick, director of the Bethlehem Public Library in Delmar, New York, considered a number of different items for a digital collection, he was looking for something that couldn't be found anywhere else. The library has a number of older books but these materials were not unique, and as Kirkpatrick explained, if the collection was destroyed they could "call Baker and Taylor and say, 'give us a new book collection' and most of it would be replicated very easily, but there are some things that just aren't and you need to focus on that." He also considered large books of county property records. The documents themselves were physically impressive, large volumes of county plats, but again, these were not unique since the county clerk also had a copy. For Bethlehem Public Library there were two important factors under consideration; what materials were unique and what the library had an obligation to preserve. Two items stood out as being hyper-local and of strong interest to genealogists and the community: a newspaper titled *The Spotlight*, and a collection of high school yearbooks.

The library had several copies of most years of the local high school yearbook, the *Oriole*, going back to 1929. The project at first seemed overwhelming in size, but for several years volunteers have been scanning and indexing one volume at a time and now there are over sixty years' worth of the books online. The yearbooks are searchable by name, and search results are linked directly to the pages where the name appears. Users who once would have needed to browse through years of books can now locate their own image or that of family or friends within a few seconds. This has been of great use to those who no longer live in the area or state. One woman had been hoping to find a photo of her father who died when she was a child. She didn't live in the state and was unsure of when he worked for the school. Before the collection was digitized the library staff had been unable to locate the correct book. Once the documents were scanned and described, however, she was able to quickly locate his photo.

Free Yearbook Scanning

Scanning documents can be expensive, but a number of libraries are now using a service from the Oklahoma Correctional Industries (OCI) to scan their yearbooks. This department of the Oklahoma Department of Corrections employs 1,499 offenders in a number of industries including metal fabrication, furniture, clothing, and records conversion and scanning. The scanning service is offered for free to schools and libraries to assist in the preservation of local, historic documents. The service showcases the work done by OCI and generates goodwill. OCI pays for shipping the books to and from the Oklahoma facilities and ensures the materials are returned to the library in the same condition as received.

Carolyn Tremblay, a reference librarian at Dover Public Library in New Hampshire, learned about OCI's Yearbook Project from the *Swiss Army Librarian* blog where an e-mail had been posted outlining the services OCI offered, including free digitization and the creation of digital files that the library was free to use however they wished.[6] The Dover Public Library established contact with OCI and put the digitization project in motion. The library received packing labels, packed the books with inventory lists, and sent them to OCI. Around five weeks later the books were returned in the same condition along with ten DVDs containing the digital copies. As a result of this program the library was able to offer the community digital access to a popular collection at limited cost to the library and without adding to the workload of an already busy staff. The paper collection was also less likely to be targeted by former students, armed with scissors, seeking to remove their photograph from specific yearbooks.

The Nicholas County Public Library in Kentucky has a collection of newspapers it scanned itself with a micro-format scanner, but the library also took advantage of OCI's services. Although originally hesitant about the free service, the library did send its yearbooks and has made the resulting files, dating back to 1948, available through its website. The collection is presented as a series of files organized into a range of years.

The files are not searchable but are available for browsing. Each page is a separate file and each image is in color with enough detail that the texture of the paper and the pores of real leather and fabric of the fake leather covers is presented. Although some websites may be more visually appealing or more complex, this library's web page offers a simple form of digital access to users.

Newspapers

Local newspapers are an important source of information for current and future researchers. If your collection is only available as original paper in either bound or loose form, it can be damaged as the paper becomes brittle over time or it may suffer from patrons who remove articles. Microfilm created before 1980 can also degrade over time, it is more difficult to use compared to electronic documents, and its use is limited to institutions with micro-format readers.

Digitization can be part of a larger strategy (with micro-formats) to preserve and improve access and discovery of the detailed depictions of daily life found in local newspapers. In January 1960 a boy stole twenty-nine light bulbs from an outdoor tree; a color film of an all-girl safari was shown at Bethlehem Central Junior High school to support multiple sclerosis research; a new library card program was being implemented at the library; and a 1956 Ford cost $895. These details of town life were found in the January 7, 1960 volume of *The Spotlight*.

When the Bethlehem Public Library was considering digitization of *The Spotlight*, theft was a significant issue. According to Frank Somers, adult services librarian, "When the newspapers were on the public floor people were going to the bound volumes and cutting out articles and pictures . . . and we wanted to protect them from that." As the only repository for these papers, the library felt responsible for preserving and providing access to the newspapers. Preserving *The Spotlight* required scanning of the paper for a microfilm copy and the creation of an electronic version. This required special equipment the library did not have. The scanning work was outsourced and paid for through funding from the Friends of the Library and from a local nonprofit organization that dissolved and donated its remaining funding to the library. *The Spotlight* is still a functioning newspaper and the owners supported the library's efforts.

The newspaper, which started in the mid-1950s as a circular, had been of interest to local genealogists and historians. For years the obituaries, wedding announcements, and articles were used but had never been digitized and *The Spotlight* was not available in any database. With no other copies in existence, the need to preserve these materials was strong.

The Spotlight is now only published in digital format and the library still works to preserve access. Regarding the new format, Somers found the publisher happy to send PDFs of the current paper and "they maintain the copyright but they were very willing to let us share the newspaper." The publishers understand that there may be people who do not respect their copyright, but they feel the risk of sharing the content online is acceptable if it results in the community having access to an important historical resource. The library is providing access to current issues of the newspaper up to one year after the original publication date.

The materials chosen for digitization are unique to the Bethlehem Public Library, and as Library Director Geoff Kirkpatrick stated "there is no one else who is going to preserve these hyper-local resources." These efforts are appreciated by users inside and outside of the local community, including the newspaper's owners, who appreciate the access and the publicity that comes from working with the library.

Newspaper Partnerships

The Bethlehem Public Library was able to work with the owners in a manner that has allowed the library to continue to preserve the newspaper while respecting the copyright and distribution needs of the owners. Newspapers and magazines published after 1923 may still have copyright limitations or may have been digitized by another institution. A number of libraries have participated in the Library of Congress's Chronicling America project, which includes newspapers from around the country spanning the years 1836 to 1922. Users can access 1,770 newspapers on the Chronicling America website. The collection is produced by the National Digital Newspaper Program and the Library of Congress. Funding is provided by the National Endowment for the Humanities. It should be noted that this is not a complete collection of American newspapers, and while participating libraries are given funding to digitize 100,000 pages, there are many papers and date ranges that are not included. An important feature within the Chronicling America website is the newspaper title directory of over 140,000 titles created through a national program to locate and create records for newspapers held by libraries around the country. The directory offers information on digitized and non-digitized papers and the libraries which house the materials. A directory of the U.S. Newspaper Program Participants provides information on the digitized material, the library that received the grant, and the amount of funds received.

Many states have "memory" projects where libraries collaborate to create an online repository of materials. Most of these projects are hosted by state-level agencies such as archives, universities, and collaborative library groups. These should be referenced before starting a newspaper digitization project. In many states successful newspaper digitization projects are the result of collaboration with multiple agencies or institutions, but there are many public libraries which have a collection which is not attached to a larger project, such as the Jefferson Parish Library's collection of the daily French language newspaper, the *New Orleans Bee* (1827–1925).[7] Other resources to search before beginning a newspaper digitization project are the Digitization Projects Registry (a Federal Depository Library Program resource), Internet Archive, and Google News Archive. The Google News Archive will now only search news for the last thirty days, but there is also a list of hundreds of digitized newspapers from *L'Abeille de la Nouvelle-Orleans* (1862–1870) to the *Youngstown Evening Vindicator* (1891–1893). This list of resources is an index of digitized newspapers from free and subscription sites compiled by Google and unveiled in 2006.[8] These newspapers are no longer searchable through the general Google News search box but can be accessed by entering the URL (news.google.com/newspapers) or searching for "Google historic newspapers."

Oral Histories

People in your local community are also wonderful and unique sources of local history, and many libraries are including oral histories in their digital collections by either converting older recordings on cassette tapes to digital media or recording new oral histories. If the condition of cassettes or reel-to-reel oral histories is a concern, digitization is an initial step in a long-term strategy to preserve those stories for future generations. Magnetic tape, when properly stored, can last for thirty years.[9] For cassettes or videotapes which were originally produced in the 1970s and 1980s, digitization may be the only way to save these materials.

When Arizona celebrated its statehood centennial, the state library encouraged libraries to contribute to the Arizona Centennial Legacy Projects. These projects were under the Arizona Centennial Commission (ACC), which was established by an executive order from the governor, and sought to "accurately portray a significant aspect of Arizona history."[10] The ACC worked with the Arizona Historical Advisory Commission to organize centennial projects with a goal of having "all 22 tribes, 15 counties and 120 cities and towns represented with at least one officially designated Arizona Centennial Event and/ or Legacy Project that is unique and meaningful to its community."[11] These projects documented ranchers, sports, women, Latino contributions, African Americans, schools, individuals, and artists. The Pima County Public Library responded to this call with a proposal to record oral histories of centenarians. The library felt that collecting stories of some of the people who were present during territorial days or the beginnings of statehood was an excellent way to mark the state's 100-year anniversary.

Although images and written documents are important links to the past, oral histories provide a different level of connection. The people who collect the stories reach out to the community, and the interview subjects share a glimpse of their lives with others. Jen Maney of the Pima County Public Library recalled, "We recruited people who were thoroughly old and for the most part we went to them and interviewed them in their homes or wherever they were." Staff were available, some of whom spoke Spanish, to facilitate the interviews and make copies of any images provided. The stories of a local community are likely personal and detailed and offer narratives of daily life by regular people. Celebrities may have their stories told in many forums, but Oscar Montono's tale of working through the Great Depression and serving in the signal corps, or Dolores Celaya's stories of making candy from cactus and life on the ranch, are only found in the oral histories collected by the Pima County Public Library. Oral histories provide first-person perspectives of civil rights struggles, war, and other topics with a variety of detail and insight which make these stories a truly unique resource.

Preserving Oral Histories

The Houston Metropolitan Research Center of the Houston Public Library is an example of an organization that successfully digitized over 200 oral histories from the 1970s and 1980s as part of a larger Houston Oral History Project. The collection at the Houston Public Library contained hundreds of audio recordings dating back to the 1970s. This collection of interviews consists of physical formats that have limited life spans and are already in the process of degrading, including cassettes and reel-to-reel analog audiotape. To preserve and provide access to these materials, about five years ago the library sought to have them digitized and hosted online.

The collection contains stories of civil rights struggles, sports, theaters, schools, and politics. According to Roland Lemonius, digital projects manager, the funding to create what would become the Houston Oral History Project came "through competitive grants and other funding sources."[12] Working with the Soundsafe Archive, an archival audio service now known as the George Blood Audio/Video, the library was able to have a large number of recordings converted. Multiple copies in different formats were generated, including CDs to extend the life of the recordings. The company provided multiple file types including CDs, MP3 files, and preservation-level master WAV files. With these different formats, Lemonius found that "we were able to create streaming media in order to make the recordings available online on our digital assets catalog."[13]

The library promotes the continued acquisition of oral histories as well as preservation. The website warns that "if we do not collect and preserve those memories, those stories, then one day they will disappear forever."[14] The digitization process results in more than just transferring the audio signal recording from a degrading reel of tape; it also ensures preservation of and continued access to the experiences of people captured on those recordings.

ORGANIZATION AND DESCRIPTION OF THE COLLECTION

A significant amount of the daily work performed by librarians, archivists, and museum staff involves the organization and description of materials. In the case of digitization projects the materials selected for digitization may need item-level description. For example, a library's collection might include a filing cabinet of pamphlets arranged alphabetically by title but never fully cataloged, or materials missed when the catalog went electronic that are still located via a card catalog. Good organization and description are key for efficient digital projects. The existence of an index, cataloging records, or finding aids makes creating additional metadata much easier. If the time needed for cataloging is an issue, identifying materials for digitization that will require less effort to process and describe will save time and frustration. The amount and type of metadata to include is another factor to consider. Digital materials require different metadata from tangible materials. This information can be included in a traditional record by incorporating links, but there are standards and schema which have been developed for different kinds of digital media and digital collections. You will also want to consider how and where you will make your digital collection available. Often, your metadata choices will be limited by the method which you chose to make your digitized items available online.

There are a number of standards you can reference for the collection of this data, and these can differ depending on the format of the material. These standards include RDA, Metadata Encoding & Transmission Standard (METS), and Visual Resources Association Core (VRA). A number of different metadata standards are being used by digital repositories based on the type of files (images, sound, moving images). These standards may incorporate a specific metadata schema or can be broadly applied to different schemas.

Starting with an Organized Collection

The Chelsea District Library in Michigan created an obituary database based on the physical index cards produced by a local genealogist, Harold A. Jones, who had partly compiled the cards by recording information from the tombstones in the local cemetery. The content of the index dates back to the founding of the community in 1834. When Jones died in 1987, the majority of his collection was gifted to the library.[15] Over two years (2002–2004) an ambitious volunteer updated and reorganized the files.[16] The index was arranged by name and cross-referenced to include women by their maiden names. Attached to some of the index cards are obituary clippings or newspaper notices, many of which were also scanned. As a tangible object, the collection of 50,000 cards was ripe for transformation into an online database.

The library staff worked with genealogists to determine the database fields that should be created to enhance searching, including fields such as parents, children, cemetery, and obituary source. Understanding that there could be other information that could potentially be useful, library staff designed the database to include a notes field where additional information could be added and this "proved to be invaluable for later expansion."[17] Over fifty volunteers entered information into the database and now a few volunteers continue to add new obituaries. The collection, formally named the Obituary File and now titled the Family History Index, presents the content of each card in a manner reproducing the appearance of the original index card.

Organizing a collection in advance of digitization reduces the amount of work required when entering metadata or deciding on an arrangement. In addition, organizing materials by type or size reduces the amount of time needed to adjust scanner settings and can result in more efficient digitization workflows.

Comes with Its Own Ascension Numbers

Collections that are already organized and described may save staff and volunteer time by reducing the need to research and identify the content of specific items. When Craig Scott at the Gadsden Public Library in Alabama received the photograph collection of Bobby Scarboro, the donation of over 4,500 images came with their own organization and descriptive system. Located on the edge or back of individual photographs was a number that often was related to a note with more information. Scott describes the nature of this descriptive information as ranging from "basically nothing, maybe a word or two" to very descriptive. Because each image already had a unique number the system was preserved in the metadata generated by staff. The numbers provided by the creator allowed for library staff to maintain the connections between the photographs and the metadata, as well as reduce the chances of misidentification.

An example of these images is one called "Hill City Boat." Under the image of a long riverboat on a foggy fall day is a handwritten note identifying the thin man in the foreground as Captain William (Bill) Elliott. On the far right of the image is a small label reading "Scarboro Photo Shop, Gadsden, Ala, R-1112."[18] This information on the image provides important identifying information for the patron and cataloger who would also recognize that the "R" in the code most likely refers to an image of the river. If there are two images with the same title the reference numbers help to differentiate the images and can be used to accurately refer to the specific photograph. If your materials are already organized and have a reliable number system it can save a considerable amount of time to utilize that system.

Subject-Based Organization

When Janis Arquette, the local history assistant at the Bensenville Community Public Library in Illinois, started her library's digital collection she developed local categories based on the photographs' subject matter. Arquette divided the collection of 300 photographs into categories based on common elements, such as if the main subject was a school, church, or person. One category she developed was "used to be" for buildings which had been destroyed. This type of division can be especially useful when paired with good metadata.

Although there were no indexes, there were descriptive materials for the collection in the form of a book of local history that provided the basis for the digital collection. Many of the images in the collection had been used in the book or were copied from it and include a page number and a quote of the text. The original book did not have an index, and Arquette created one to act as a finding aid for both the book and online collection. Between the book, which organized Bensenville history into subjects such as schools and churches, and the categorization scheme that arose as she looked through the photographs for common themes, Arquette was able to organize the collection. The resulting digital collection has a unique visual presentation. The first image users see is a drawing of the historic Korthauer house, which is owned by the library and the local historical society. Instead of a list of subjects or collections, the Bensenville collection is presented with an image of a living room with the furnishing as links to specific areas of the collections. Clicking on the fireplace takes the user to materials relating to the fire department, schools are found by clicking on the pile of wooden blocks, and the quilt hanging on the wall leads to quilt squares created for the nation's centennial. Those squares that depict buildings are linked to photographs of the same building and location. Images and text are presented in a narrative format rather than a catalog record.

The Bensenville collection is hosted by the library. This gives the library considerable control over the presentation and organization of the materials. Because the library hosts the site, they must also maintain the files and links. Arquette has some training on how to maintain the site, but over time she lost the ability to make changes and fix broken links. Until the library is able to find another IT person the links may remain broken.

If your library is interested in creating a digital collection, look for themes in the material which will help you organize the items. Finding aids or local history may provide additional information or suggest a method of organization. If you are uncomfortable maintaining a website, consider having your material added to a larger collection such as a state or regional digital collection. Hosted sites will reduce the amount of effort necessary to maintain a site but may have a required level of metadata. CONTENTdm sites use Dublin Core schema and the presentation of the metadata is concise, with searchable subject keywords. With this schema the library can goes beyond the fifteen core elements and include the names of private contributors; whether the materials are privately owned; project information if the digitizing was tied to a grant; and decade information. Descriptive metadata can still be evocative, but the presentation is standardized. Having this type of metadata also aids in maintaining files. Should the digitized image be damaged or lost the library will be able to easily locate their master copy.

SIZE MATTERS

When choosing a collection for digitization it is important to consider the size of the material both in quantity, physical size, and format. It will potentially take less time to digitize a few photographs than a shelf of genealogies or a full run of magazines. Depending on a library's resources, the digitization work could be performed by volunteers or outsourced to a digitization vendor. In addition, equipment is currently available that is able to scan microfilmed newspapers at high speeds that are more efficient than scanning individual pages of paper versions.

Murals, posters, paintings, and other large objects will require different equipment than a desktop scanner. The collection of World War I and World War II posters at the Bangor Public Library in Maine required a special vacuum table and a digital photographer to create accurate copies without damaging the original posters. If your library does not have the equipment or staff to digitize a large collection, outsourcing may be an option. Sending microfilmed newspapers to be scanned is a common practice.

Once the collection is digitized the resulting digital files will need to be stored. Digital collections require storage, and external storage services may have limits on the number of items or the amount of data storage space available. Alabama Mosaic's community space was able to host the Gadsden Public Library's collection of photographs from Bobby Scarboro, but their CON-TENTdm collection was limited to 10,000 items.

CASE STUDY

A COLLECTION IN DELTA CITY

Delta City, Utah, has a population of 3,436 and is a little west of dead center of the state of Utah.[19] The city is home to the Great Basin Museum and the Topaz Museum, which has a collection of art and artifacts relating to a World War II internment camp for ethnic Japanese. Outside of the city are rich fossil beds of trilobites and a marker indicating the site of explorer John Williams Gunnison's death in 1853. Founded in 1907, the city is in the high desert, flat and arid, but the Gunnison Bend Reservoir provides water for the alfalfa fields and dairies surrounding the city. The local economy is supported by a coal power plant and a beryllium mine and the area is rich with other minerals including red beryl (a rare ruby-like gem), geodes, and obsidian.

The town's library is in a one-story L-shaped building that is also the location of the police department and city hall. In front of the library a bronze sculpture of Mark Twain sits on a bench as if waiting to read a story to someone. Inside the building are eight computers for public use and over 32,000 books. The regular schedule of events includes story time and a Legos club where children work on building projects based on books. The library is doing well, with an annual circulation total of almost 33,000 items. The library has one librarian, Deborah B. Greathouse, and a total staff of five people. Their budget is about $147,000.[20] Despite not having a website until fairly recently, the library has established an impressive digitization program.

The digitization program started in 2007–2008 with a grant from the Utah State Library and the University of Utah, which at the time was the only Utah facility to have digitization equipment. All the grants for the library's digitization projects were written by library director Deborah Greathouse. These include a grant to hire a person to create metadata for an important selection of photographs comprising the Frank Beckwith Collection.

The Beckwith Collection

Scrapbooks are a popular item for digitization due to their rich, unique, and personal content. For the Delta City Library the scrapbooks, articles, glass plate negatives, and photos created by Frank Asahel Beckwith were just a starting point. Beckwith had been an amateur geologist, anthropologist, and the editor and publisher of the *Millard County Chronicle* from 1919 to 1951. Events that Beckwith documented include the construction of the Deseret Melville Abraham and Delta Dam in 1919, which provided water for agriculture and later a power plant. Cultural aspects of the area are recorded in photographs Beckwith captured of petroglyphs, Native American artifacts, homes, Native Americans, and Utah landscapes. The images show the development of the area and the daily lives of residents, from livestock shows in 1954 to floods in 1983. These images are primarily black and white but are full of local color. The project also included digitizing the local newspaper owned by the Beckwith family up to the 1940s. The director of the library is a member of the Beckwith family and had access to many photographs family members had taken while working on newspaper stories. This led to a collection documenting marriages, births, deaths, and other events in the community, including descriptive information for each photograph. The collection is unique to Delta City and full of local interest.

One of the important aspects of this collection was the fact that the materials were already organized. Images taken for the newspaper were accompanied by descriptions, names, and dates as would be found in a newspaper article. Names are provided with positions (left to right), and captions give locations and events (for example, Sevier River Flood, of 1983). The scrapbooks were scanned with the pages intact and dedicated to specific subjects and locations. Many contained title pages with dates, narratives, and the names of photographers with some of the images. The description for one reads "Scrapbook by Frank A. Beckwith describing Arches National Monument, providing the reader with a tour of the area as it was in the 1930s; includes photographs."[21] All this information accompanying the collection made the recording of metadata much easier than if the cataloger had to identify the people and places with assistance.

Marketing the Collection

To promote access to this material locally, advertisements were placed in the local newspaper. These ads were useful for heightening interest in the project and have increased access to general history and genealogy resources. People within the local community and outside of it have been able to find family photos, and the Bureau of Land Management has used the images created by Frank Beckwith to document Indian petroglyphs. Brigham Young University used two images from the collection in a documentary; publisher Gibbs Smith included one of the library's images in a fourth-grade textbook; and requests to use images have come from as far away as the College of William & Mary in Virginia.

Beckwith Was Just the Beginning

The success of the Beckwith project led to more grants and more historic information being made available to the public. Additional grant funding in 2009 and 2013 led to the digitization of over 5,000 pages of the *Millard County Chronicle*, extending the holdings from 1910 to 1947. Usage of the newspaper collection increased 13 percent with these additional materials. In a 2013 LSTA grant proposal Greathouse wrote "The back issues of the *Millard County Chronicle* are not easily accessible to the public after 1943. People have to call the newspaper office and have them do research or try and find the microfilm;

either way this process is time consuming and tedious."[22] The grant awarded $6,956 to the library.[23]

Newspapers tend to be organized by title and date. The collection of the *Millard County Chronicle* includes individual articles and advertisements within the paper. A user may open an edition and see the title of each article which appears on a page.

Greathouse also contacted local families to acquire additional photographs, which resulted in another eighty images being added to the collection. This local history collection has drawn interest from other states, including a man from Arizona who found a photograph of his parents, siblings, nieces, and nephews that he had never seen before.[24] A real estate broker used the collection to help a home-buyer looking to convert a school into a home, and a researcher in Pasadena, California was able to (with the assistance of the library staff) find an article on a Utah archeologist. These newspapers are available on the Utah Digital Newspapers website.

The digitization of the Beckwith images was completed in 2011, but other efforts are ongoing. The local museum is loaning materials for digitization, and the current challenge is finding more material to add to the digital collection. Greathouse intends to add to the newspaper collection and have the *Millard County Chronicle* scanned from 1948 to 1953. Another step for the library is to create a policy for use of images now that more agencies and individuals are able to access the collections and are interested in using images for various projects. ▪■▪

Chapter Synopsis

The reasons for creating your collection will have a strong influence on how you proceed with your project:

- **Preservation:** file size, type, storage, and how files will be maintained need to be considered before you start.
- **Access:** The level of metadata, where your collection will be located, and how users will find your collection should be considered before you scan.
- **Complete or growing:** Will your project reach a point of completion or is it a growing collection? If the materials you are digitizing are for a specific event, consider whether or not you want to provide perpetual access to those materials. Growing collections will need attention and have increasing space requirements.

When choosing the collection ask yourself:

- Is it unique? If your library is the only source for this material, you may feel obligated to protect and provide access.
- Is there interest? Hyper-local materials tend to be unique in nature. No other library will have images of Nesqually Canoe Journeys or Beckwith's photos of weddings and rodeos. Your library may be the only source for back issues of your local newspaper.
- Find a collection that resonates with your community. It may be the collection of a local photographer, a beloved newspaper columnist, or a collection of obituaries. Look for newspapers, photographs, or other material that would benefit from easier access. Consider materials that document recent events.
- Is it organized? Collections that are already organized or have a guide to help arrange the materials should be considered. Materials which already have some form of metadata will save time and effort in the process of creating your database.
- How large will the collection be? If the material you are digitizing is in a large format or will require a significant amount of digital space, you may need new equipment or you may need to outsource the digitization of the materials. Consider your options for digital storage and if you will have the room and budget to store the items you plan to scan.

NOTES

1. Jennie Appelman, 1930s, photograph, "Billings—Images of People," Montana Memory Project, Billings, MT, http://cdm103401.cdmhost.com/cdm/singleitem/collection/p103401pblhc/id/408/rec/1.
2. *Clay County Advocate-Press*, "Obituary: Charles E. Overstreet, 88," December 9, 2010, www.advocatepress.com/article/20101209/News/312099886.
3. Mark Lambird, "Charles Overstreet, February 12, 1922–December 7, 2010," *Clay County Advocate-Press*, December 9, 2010.
4. "The Canoe Journeys ~ A Nisqually Perspective," Washington Rural Heritage, www.washingtonruralheritage.org/cdm/about/collection/nisqually.
5. Arwyn Rice, "Tribal Canoe Journeys on Hiatus in 2015 after No Host Comes Forward," *Peninsula Daily News*, September 16, 2014, www.peninsuladailynews.com/article/20140917/NEWS/309179990.

6. Brian Herzog, "The Yearbook Project from OCI," *Swiss Army Librarian*, November 20, 2013, www.swissarmylibrarian.net/2013/11/20/the-yearbook-project-from-oci/.

7. Genealogy, *New Orleans Bee*, Jefferson Parish Library. www.jefferson.lib.la.us/genealogy/NewOrleansBeeMain.htm.

8. John Markoff, "Google to Offer Print-Archives Searches," *New York Times,* September 6, 2006, www.nytimes.com/2006/09/06/business/media/06google.html.

9. Jean-Louis Bigourdan, James M. Reilly, Karen Santoro, and Gene Salesin, *The Preservation of Magnetic Tape Collections: A Perspective* (Rochester, NY: Image Permanence Institute, Rochester Institute of Technology, 2006), 6, https://www.imagepermanenceinstitute.org/webfm_send/303.

10. Arizona Centennial Legacy Projects, Arizona State Library, Archives & Public Records, https://www.azlibrary.gov/sites/azlibrary.gov/files/ahac-legacy-projects.pdf.

11. "About," AZ100years.com, www.az100years.org/about/.

12. Roland Lemonius, personal e-mail with the author, January 8, 2015.

13. Ibid.

14. "How to Create an Oral History of Your Own," Houston Oral History Project, www.houstonoralhistory.org/create.html.

15. Elizabeth Goldman, "Digitization on a Dime: How a Small Library and a Big Team of Volunteers Digitized 15,000 Obituaries in Just Over a Year," in *Digitization in the Real World,* ed. Kwong Bor Ng and Jason Kucsma (Metropolitan New York Library Council, 2010).

16. "Family History Index," Chelsea District Library, http://storiesofchelsea.chelsea districtlibrary.org/?page_id=2995.

17. Goldman, "Digitization on a Dime," 50.

18. *Hill City Boat,* photograph, Scarboro Collection, Gadsden Public Library, http://digital.archives.alabama.gov/cdm/singleitem/collection/gpl01/id/2097.

19. Delta City, Utah, DP-1 U.S. Profile of General Population and Housing Characteristics: 2010, U.S. Census Bureau, 2010 Census.

20. Delta Public Library, Public Libraries Survey, Fiscal Year 2012, Institute of Museum and Library Services.

21. "Arches National Monument scrapbook," J. Willard Marriott Library website, http://content.lib.utah.edu/cdm/ref/collection/DC_Beckwith/id/2744.

22. Deb Greathouse, "Application for 2013 LSTA Grant," 2013.

23. "2013 LSTA Sub-Grant Award Recipients," Utah Department of Heritage and the Arts, http://heritage.utah.gov/wp-content/uploads/USL-2013-LSTA-Grant-Award-Recipients.pdf.

24. Deb Greathouse, "Project Report," 2010.

CHAPTER 2

DIGITIZING COPYRIGHTED MATERIALS

If it is difficult for you to find a rights holder after employing due diligence, it ought to be equally difficult for a claimant to show that a copyright had been secured.

—Library of Congress[1]

Before initiating a digitization project, it is important to ensure that the library has the right to digitize the material.[2] Some materials may be protected by copyright while others are not and are part of the public domain. Original documents donated to your library may have included different permissions and restrictions on use. Some material may have been in the collection for so long that there is no longer any documentation regarding permissions on usage. Do your current donation forms include language regarding copyright, permissions, and digitization? Perceived legal problems within the scope of copyright law can keep some libraries from even attempting a project. There are helpful sources and tools you can use to get a better understanding of copyright law and how it affects your digitization project. The following gives an overview of copyright law, important exceptions to copyright law—such as the doctrine of fair use and public domain materials—along with some tips on managing copyright affairs within a digitization project.

WHAT IS COPYRIGHT?

Copyright law in the United States protects an author's original expression of creative work so that they are able to financially benefit from it for a limited period of time. After such period of time has ended the work is no longer covered by copyright and falls into the public domain. The foundations of U.S. copyright law are based on British law, as well as on the first article of the U.S. Constitution: [3]

> The Congress shall have Power . . . to promote the Progress of Science and useful Arts by securing for limited Times to Authors and Inventors exclusive Right to their respective Writings and Discoveries. [4]

WHAT KINDS OF WORKS DOES COPYRIGHT PROTECT?

Current copyright law protects the following kinds of works so long as they are "fixed in any tangible medium of expression." [5]

- Literary works
- Musical works (including accompanying words)
- Dramatic works (including accompanying music)
- Pantomimes and choreographic works
- Pictorial, graphic, and sculptural works
- Motion pictures and other audiovisual works
- Sound recordings
- Architectural works [6]

Copyright does not protect ideas, facts, theories, titles, brief phrases, names, or processes. Any fixed expression of an idea, theory, or process can be copyrighted; for instance, a painting or a scientific article about the Big Bang theory has copyright protection. The actual theory is not protected by copyright. It is also helpful to know that copyright does not protect works created by U.S. federal government agencies.

DOES A WORK NEED TO BE SIGNED OR REGISTERED IN ORDER TO BE COPYRIGHTED?

It is important to note that copyright protects a work as soon as it is created. No notice of any kind, or formal registration with the U.S. Copyright Office (USCO) is required for a work to be copyrighted. However, formal registration carries benefits that assist an author in court if they decide to sue another party for copyright infringement. Registration with the USCO establishes prima facie evidence to a court that the author possesses copyright in the work. It also allows the author to sue for statutory damages rather than actual damages in an infringement lawsuit; statutory damages can range from $750 to $150,000 per infringed work.[7]

Consider the federal court case *Capitol Records, Inc. v. Thomas-Rasset,* which lasted from 2007 until 2012. Jammie Thomas-Rasset was found guilty of copyright infringement for illegally downloading and file-sharing twenty-four popular songs. The plaintiffs, because these twenty-four songs were registered with the U.S. Copyright Office in their name, were awarded statutory damages—$9,250 per song—rather than actual damages which could have been much smaller; for example, think of the cost of an iTunes download or an entire CD at a store.[8]

WHAT RIGHTS DO COPYRIGHT OWNERS HAVE?

Authors, artists, musicians, choreographers, and other creators (hereby referred to as "authors" in a general sense) have the following six exclusive rights in their copyrighted works:

- Reproduce or copy the work.
- Create derivative works based on the work (e.g., a movie based on a book)
- Distribute copies of the work by selling it, lending it, renting it, or otherwise transferring it.
- Publicly performing the work.
- Publicly displaying the work.
- Digitally transmitting the work as a sound recording.[9]

These rights are not without exceptions. In order to maintain the free flow of creativity and ideas in a democratic society, as well as to ensure that copyright does not impinge upon others' freedom of speech, the copyright law contains a handful of exceptions.[10]

WHO USUALLY OWNS COPYRIGHT IN DONATIONS TO BE DIGITIZED?

The six exclusive rights of copyright owners are a bundle of rights that can be transferred. While it may seem obvious that the creator of a copyrightable work is the rights holder, the reality is that creators may transfer some or all of their rights to others. For instance, an author may give an exclusive license to his or her publisher to copy and distribute their book, but the author retains all other rights. An employee taking photos or creating other works in the course of her job may transfer all of her rights according to her employment policies or contracts (also known as work for hire). There may be more than one copyright holder in some works; a book may have two authors or a work of art may have more than one artist assisting in its creation. Another example of this manifests itself within sound and video recordings. There can be numerous copyright owners in either medium, which can make the permissions process complex.[11]

Donors may wish to give you all kinds of materials for a potential digitization project such as photographs, scrapbooks, recorded interviews, or performances. Your library may also wish to embark on an oral history project. In terms of those materials which are still covered by copyright, who owns the rights in these works?

Photographs

Despite the myth that subjects in a photo have the copyright to the work, it is usually the one who takes the photo who owns it. Another copyright myth around photographs is that if the library owns the physical photograph then it owns the copyright; this is definitely not the truth any more than it is for books or other materials in one's collection. In professionally taken photos or portraits, the photographer or the studio owns the copyright. In personal photographs, whoever took the photo owns the copyright.[12]

Oral Histories or Interviews

If a release form was not signed, the interviewee typically owns the copyright in a recorded interview. The interviewer may have copyright in his or her recorded questions. This has implications for oral history projects in that a library will want to have the interviewee sign a form to transfer the appropriate rights for recordings to be available on the library's website.[13]

Music Performances

Let's say that a donor wanted to give you a collection of recordings featuring the local community orchestra or high school band. Copyright and music recordings can be very complex. This is because there can be multiple rights holders in a recording; the composition being recorded as well as the recording of the performance both enjoy their own respective copyright protections.[14] The composer of the works performed, recording technician, performers, and any sponsoring institutions (such as a high school) may share copyright in the recording to some degree.[15] Sometimes licenses, contracts, or other agreements may transfer copyright in the recording to an individual, one business, or a single institution. If this is the case then locating the rights holder of the sound recording will not be as difficult; however, you will also need to locate the composer for permission.[16]

Videos

As with music, video materials can have multiple rights holders, and they are even more complex in terms of copyright. Perhaps a donor approaches you with a collection of VHS tapes of a high school's annual variety shows from the late 1980s and early 1990s. These variety shows likely contain copyrighted material such as sound recordings, performances of music, drama, and so on. On top of this would be original copyrighted works by students such as skits, comedy sketches, poetry, or their own musical compositions. One might need to seek permission to digitize the tape from a variety of rights holders.[17] Because of such complexities, tread very cautiously when considering whether or not to digitize such videos.

WHAT IS A DONOR AGREEMENT?

A donor agreement, or a deed of gift, is an agreement between the library and the donor of a collection as to how said collection will be used by the library and by patrons. It is a legal agreement between the two parties and can transfer certain legal rights to the library when it acquires the collection.[18] This is an important step to take with a donor because you will want to negotiate the right to make the collection available for use by the public as well as to digitize it. A deed of gift addresses how users will be able to access and use the collection as well as working out with the donor which parts of the collection will be kept private or eliminated from the collection based on your collection development policies.[19] It will also assist greatly if the donor is the copyright holder of the materials that they wish to donate, so that you may ask them to transfer rights needed in order to digitize the collection and make the items publicly available.

For examples of how donor agreements work with a library digitization project, Curt Witcher, genealogy center manager of the Allen County Public Library (ACPL) in Fort Wayne, Indiana, provides some insight in an interview.

The ACPL hosts the Allen County Community Album digital project. Witcher states that the ACPL uses a donor agreement which asks donors to sign an agreement giving them "perpetual, non-exclusive rights to present this material on our website."[20] Most of the time, donors have had no problems with this agreement and are happy to sign it. The only exception, Witcher stated, was a collection of photographs taken by a local theatre director. This particular donor did not want the library to make the items available to the public in any manner. ACPL did not accept the donor's collection because of these extreme restrictions on accessing the collection.[21]

HOW LONG DOES COPYRIGHT LAST?

For works created after 1978, copyright in the United States lasts for the life of the author plus seventy (70) years after their death.[22] In the case of works made for hire after 1978 copyright lasts either ninety-five (95) years after publication or 120 years after its creation.[23] If the work is unpublished and created after 1978 by an anonymous author, pseudonymous author, or it is not known whether they have died, the copyright lasts 120 years after the date of creation.[24] When copyright expires in a work, it becomes part of the public domain.

WHAT IS THE PUBLIC DOMAIN?

In addition to ideas, facts, theories, titles, brief phrases, names, processes, and works created by the U.S. federal government, the public domain contains materials that are no longer protected by copyright law. In the United States, items published prior to 1923 are in the public domain. The year 1923 is an important one to remember because of this. Any items, with the very large exception of sound recordings, published before this year can be digitized without the need for permission.[25]

Materials that have not been published have a longer duration of copyright. Any unpublished work, with the exception of sound recordings, created after 1895 is still protected by copyright. Unpublished works created by an author who died prior to 1945 are in the public domain. Works made for hire that were created prior to 1895 are also in the public domain.[26]

There is a grey area in terms of copyright duration for works published in between 1923 and 1977. When these works were created, it was necessary for them to be registered with the Copyright Office in order for them to be protected by copyright law, and the copyrights could also be renewed. If a work that you would like to digitize falls into one of these two categories then it could be in the public domain: (1) work was published with notice in between 1923 and 1963 and not renewed; or (2) work was published without notice in between 1923 and 1977.[27] It is important to look through the U.S. Copyright Office's *Catalog of Copyright Entries* for verification on whether the work was renewed or even registered through the Copyright Office. Even with such verification on a particular item, it is prudent to consult with an attorney who specializes in intellectual property law and to confirm with the Copyright Office before digitizing such a work without permission. In most cases an attorney and the Copyright Office will charge for research and consultation but it may likely be worth it in case something was amiss.

WHAT IS FAIR USE?

With respect to library digitization projects, the doctrine of fair use is likely the most important exception to the six exclusive rights of copyright holders; it is also the most misunderstood one. Fair use allows for using copyrighted material for the purposes of "criticism, comment, news reporting, teaching (including multiple copies for classroom use), scholarship, or research."[28] There are four factors within the statutory language of fair use that judges use to determine whether a use is fair in an infringement lawsuit:

(1) the *purpose* and character of the use, including whether such use is of a commercial nature or is for nonprofit educational purposes;
(2) the *nature* of the copyrighted work;
(3) the *amount* and substantiality of the portion used in relation to the copyrighted work as a whole; and
(4) the *effect* of the use upon the potential market for or value of the copyrighted work.

The fact that a work is unpublished shall not itself bar a finding of fair use if such finding is made upon consideration of all the above factors.[29]

Notice that there are no percentages, number of pages, or amounts of a copyrighted work mentioned within these four factors. There are no amounts given in the rest of the statute either. Many librarians and other educators have conflated the "Agreement on Guidelines for Classroom Copying in Not-For-Profit Educational Institutions with Respect to Books and Periodicals," "Guidelines with Respect to Music," and various other fair use guidelines with the actual statutory language of fair use. These guidelines do prescribe amounts of copyrighted works that would be considered fair uses (e.g., 10 percent of a work of prose). Such amounts were agreed upon and set into place by publisher groups, authors, educators, as well as members of Congress in 1976. However, it is important to remember that these guidelines are not actual law. These guidelines, written in the late 1970s, also do not address digitization projects.[30]

The language of the actual statute can indeed be considered vague. While this can be confusing due to lack of bright line rules in how to apply fair use to a situation, it also allows for flexibility. Outside of the "Agreement on Guidelines for Classroom Copying in Not-For-Profit Educational Institutions" there are other helpful resources to assist librarians in applying fair use for a potential digitization project. Described below are two authoritative sets of tools that were either created or spearheaded by copyright experts—often with the expertise and experiences of librarians working with fair use issues on a day-to-day basis.

The first tool, *Fair Use Checklist,* was originally created in 1998 by copyright experts Kenneth Crews and Dwayne Butler. It assists potential fair users with coming to their own conclusions about their use of copyrighted material. The checklist is arranged into four sections, which is important for helping one to remember the four factors of fair use: (1) *purpose* (of use); (2) *nature* (of copyrighted work being used); (3) *amount* (of copyrighted work used); and (4) *effect* (on market for copyrighted work). Each section then has a checklist of behaviors that are either in favor of the particular factor or oppose it. One can then balance out the positives and negatives to determine whether or not a use is fair. Using this checklist should be saved as potential evidence for a fair use defense if an institution is sued for infringement. The introduction and checklist is quoted here:

> This checklist is provided as a tool to assist you when undertaking a fair use analysis. The four factors listed in the Copyright Statute are only guidelines for making a determination as to whether a use is fair. Each factor should be given careful consideration in analyzing any specific use. There is no magic formula; an arithmetic approach to the application of the four factors should not be used. Depending on the specific facts of a case, it is possible that even if three of the factors would tend to favor a fair use finding, the fourth factor may be the most important one in that particular case, leading to a conclusion that the use may not be considered fair.

FIGURE 2.1

Fair Use Checklist by Kenneth Crews (formerly of Columbia University) and Dwayne K. Butler (University of Louisville)

FAIR USE CHECKLIST

Copyright Advisory Office, Columbia University Libraries

Kenneth D. Crews, Director   http://copyright.columbia.edu

NAME:

INSTITUTION:

PROJECT:

DATE:

PREPARED BY:

PURPOSE

FAVORING FAIR USE

- ☐ Teaching (including multiple copies for classroom use)
- ☐ Research
- ☐ Scholarship
- ☐ Nonprofit educational institution
- ☐ Criticism
- ☐ Comment
- ☐ News reporting
- ☐ Transformative or productive use (changes the work for new utility)
- ☐ Restricted access (to students or other appropriate group)
- ☐ Parody

OPPOSING FAIR USE

- ☐ Commercial activity
- ☐ Profiting from the use
- ☐ Entertainment
- ☐ Bad-faith behavior
- ☐ Denying credit to original author

NATURE

FAVORING FAIR USE

- ☐ Published work
- ☐ Factual or nonfiction based
- ☐ Important to favored educational objectives

OPPOSING FAIR USE

- ☐ Unpublished work
- ☐ Highly creative work (art, music, novels, films, plays)
- ☐ Fiction

AMOUNT

FAVORING FAIR USE

- ☐ Small quantity
- ☐ Portion used is not central or significant to entire work
- ☐ Amount is appropriate for favored educational purpose

OPPOSING FAIR USE

- ☐ Large portion or whole work used
- ☐ Portion used is central to or "heart of the to work"

EFFECT

FAVORING FAIR USE

- ☐ User owns lawfully purchased or acquired copy of original work
- ☐ One or few copies made
- ☐ No significant effect on the market or potential market for copyrighted work
- ☐ No similar product marketed by the copyright holder
- ☐ Lack of licensing mechanism

OPPOSING FAIR USE

- ☐ Could replace sale of copyrighted work
- ☐ Significantly impairs market or potential market for copyrighted work or derivative
- ☐ Reasonably available licensing mechanism for use of the copyrighted work
- ☐ Affordable permission available for using work
- ☐ Numerous copies made
- ☐ You made it accessible on the Web or in other public forum
- ☐ Repeated or long-term use

Most recent revision: 051408

The second set of tools to consider for fairly using materials for your digitization project are codes or statements of best practices in fair use. These tools were spearheaded by Pat Aufderheide, university professor, School of Communication at American University, and Peter Jaszi, professor of law and faculty director of the Glushko-Samuelson Intellectual Property Clinic at American University. The movement started in 2005 with the development of the *Documentary Filmmakers Statement of Best Practices in Fair Use.*[31] Such codes or statements of best practices in fair use are developed by user groups of copyrighted materials along with legal consultants to document common fair use behaviors. There are now a large number of disciplines and user groups who have crafted such documents, some of which can be used by public libraries to assist them in making fair use determinations when the need arises. It is still important to remember that, like the 1976 *Guidelines*, these best practices should not be viewed as the limit on what can be fairly used.[32]

The *Code of Best Practices in Fair Use for Academic and Research Libraries* was crafted by and for academic and research librarians in consultation with legal experts. These librarians agreed on eight common situations—or principles—where fair use needs to be applied in their day-to-day work or major projects. Principle four, "Creating Digital Collections of Archival and Special Collections Materials," would be most applicable to a public library's potential digitization project. With digitizing any special collection, it's important to refer to the deed of gift or any other related agreement to make sure that any donor restrictions are applicable.[33] Quoted below is the principle along with limitations and enhancements:

Principle
It is fair use to create digital versions of a library's special collections and archives and to make these versions electronically accessible in appropriate contexts.

Limitations
- Providing access to published works that are available in unused copies on the commercial market at reasonable prices should be undertaken only with careful consideration, if at all. To the extent that the copy of such a work in a particular collection is unique . . . access to unique aspects of the copy will be supportable under fair use. The presence of non-unique copies in a special collection can be indicated by descriptive entries without implicating copyright.

- Where digitized special collections are posted online, reasonable steps should be taken to limit access to material likely to contain damaging or sensitive private information.
- Full attribution, in a form satisfactory to scholars in the field, should be provided for all special collection items made available online, to the extent it is reasonably possible to do so.

Enhancements

- The fair use case will be even stronger where items to be digitized consist largely of works, such as personal photographs, correspondence, or ephemera, whose owners are not exploiting the material commercially and likely could not be located to seek permission for new uses.
- Libraries should consider taking technological steps, reasonable in light of both the nature of the material and of institutional capabilities, to prevent downloading of digital files by users, or else limit the quality of files to what is appropriate to the use.
- Libraries should also provide copyright owners with a simple tool for registering objections to online use, and respond to such objections promptly.
- Subject to the considerations outlined above, a special collection should be digitized in its entirety, and presented as a cohesive collection whenever possible.
- Adding criticism, commentary, rich metadata, and other additional value and context to the collection will strengthen the fair use case.
- The fair use case will be stronger when the availability of the material is appropriately publicized to scholars in the field and other persons likely to be especially interested.[34]

Both the *Fair Use Checklist* and the *Code of Best Practices* can assist a public library in coming to its own conclusions about how fair use can apply to a digitization project, as well as crafting a starting point for copyright policy in digitization projects. It is important that a library evaluate a project on all four factors of fair use and not make an assumption that just because it may be a nonprofit educational institution that fair use will always apply to using copyrighted works. One needs to apply both sets of tools to each individual new project. Each new project that has the potential to employ fair use with respect to using copyrighted materials needs to be reevalluated *de novo* since the four factors of fair use are sensitive to specific situations.[35]

WHAT IS THE LIBRARIES AND ARCHIVES EXCEPTION?

17 U.S.C. Sec. 108 is the "libraries and archives exception" within American copyright law. It's important to note, however, that this section deals more with preservation than with making library materials available in a digitization project. A fair amount of this statute is out of date with respect to current technologies and ways that copyrighted materials are distributed. However, the last portion of the statute—17 U.S.C. Sec. 108(h)—is the most relevant to a digitization project:

> (h) (1) For purposes of this section, during the last 20 years of any term of copyright of a published work, a library or archives, including a nonprofit educational institution that functions as such, may reproduce, distribute, display, or perform in facsimile or digital form a copy or phonorecord of such work, or portions thereof, for purposes of preservation, scholarship, or research, if such library or archives has first determined, on the basis of a reasonable investigation, that none of the conditions set forth in subparagraphs (A), (B), and (C) of paragraph (2) apply.
>
> (2) No reproduction, distribution, display, or performance is authorized under this subsection if—
>   (A) the work is subject to normal commercial exploitation;
>   (B) a copy or phonorecord of the work can be obtained at a reasonable price; or
>   (C) the copyright owner or its agent provides notice pursuant to regulations promulgated by the Register of Copyrights that either of the conditions set forth in subparagraphs (A) and (B) applies.
> (3) The exemption provided in this subsection does not apply to any subsequent uses by users other than such library or archives.[36]

Using this exception only applies to published works as defined in 17 U.S.C. Sec. 101. It would be incumbent upon the library to carefully document its steps if one wished to use this part of the libraries and archives exception. Such documentation should include the following facts:

(1) the work was indeed published;
(2) it is in the last 20 years of its copyright protection;
(3) it is no longer commercially available;
(4) it is not able to be purchased at a reasonable price; and

(5) the copyright holder has not indicated with the Copyright Office that the item is commercially available.

HOW DO I GET PERMISSION TO USE A COPYRIGHTED WORK FOR MY DIGITIZATION PROJECT?

There will be times when fair use, or other exceptions to the rights of copyright holders, may not be the best thing to employ as a defense to use a copyrighted work without permission in a digitization project. At this point, one may have used a fair use checklist, and looked at guidelines or best practices, and it becomes clear that fair use would not be an option. This is when it becomes important to know the process of asking permission of rights holders in order to use an item in a digitization project.

Upon the realization that permission is needed to use a copyrighted item in a digitization project, it is important to obtain it well in advance of when the item will need to be used. Be sure to communicate with rights holders in writing so that you can keep documentation in case of any potential conflicts or miscommunications. It is also important to document your process of locating the rights holder—from phone calls to e-mails and letters sent via postal service.

Finding Rights Holders

When working with items to digitize, you will likely have unpublished items as well as published ones. For example, your library may wish to digitize high school yearbooks, which qualify as published works. Members of the respective communities you serve may wish to have you digitize their own personal photographs to document the history of your locale. Such photos, diaries, letters, and other related materials are examples of unpublished works. Lastly, donors may also wish to donate sound or video recordings. It's important to know who owns the copyright in these items so that you can contact the appropriate rights holders.

It is generally easier to find the copyright holder in items that are published rather than those that are not. In either case, to begin the process to locate rights holders, have a look at the item for any company names, copyright notices, names of photographers, artists, authors, composers, or logos. From there you will have some information to begin your search. Try searching the Internet, newspaper searches, or other historical databases to help you track down the original copyright owner and his or her heirs. Make phone calls to any companies you may see with respect to the original rights holder to make sure that you have the correct rights holder. Note that there will be times when you will not be able to locate a rights holder; sometimes copyright can be transferred to companies or multiple heirs without any easily traceable documentation. Other times a search may not turn up a verified copyright owner—more on this later.[37] There are several sources that can help you verify rights holders on items you wish to digitize:

Catalog of Copyright Entries (http://archive.org/details/copyrightrecords): When researching the rights holder for an item created prior to 1978, one can look at digitized copies of the *Catalog of Copyright Entries*. Currently the Internet Archive has volumes going back to 1891. You'll need to use other search engines in order to possibly locate contact information for the rights holder.

ASCAP and BMI (https://www.ascap.com/Home/ace-title-search/index .aspx) & (http://repertoire.bmi.com/artistSearch.asp): These two organizations are related to composers and musicians. Both are collective licensing organizations where you can contact one or the other to seek permission—or a license—to use a musical score. The organization then charges you a fee to use the work and forwards the royalties on to the author. You can use the links above to search for a rights holder related to a score. If you found the work that you'd like to use, then you can make a request to license the work from the organization. It is important to note that these organizations do not handle rights for sound recordings of a musical work, however.

Recording Industry Association of America and Harry Fox Agency: Sound recordings of musical works can become complex when investigating rights holders. Oftentimes there are two sets of copyright holders you need to keep in mind with sound recordings: (1) the rights holder of the musical score; and (2) the rights holder of the sound recording. The two organizations listed above can be helpful for locating the rights holders of a sound recording.

Copyright Clearance Center (www.copyright.com): The Copyright Clearance Center is another collective licensing organization that works mainly with book and journal article content. If the copyright holder works with CCC it will be relatively easy to request a license to use the work.

Artists' Rights Society (ARS) and Visual Artists and Galleries Association (VAGA): These two organizations are the main collective licensing organizations for visual artists.

Needed Details of a Letter Requesting Permission to Use a Copyrighted Item

So you've found the rights holder after a thorough search, documented your steps in finding them, and are ready to ask permission to use an item in your digitization project. How do you proceed? First, clearly convey in writing the title of the work, how much of the work you want to use, and how and why you want to use the item. Rights holders will usually only give you permission for the use that you explicitly state in writing.[38] Be sure to save copies of letters, e-mails, or copies of notes taken in your documentation. For easy reference and preservation, it helps to digitize such communications and save them on a server that is backed up very frequently. Verbiage for a permission request form letter should include (1) your name and organization, (2) the name of the rights holder, (3) complete citation of the work, (4) how you want to use the item and for what purpose, and (5) asking the party to forward you to the appropriate people if they are not able to grant permission.[39]

What Happens If I Never Hear from (or Find) the Copyright Owner?

Sometimes, after all of the work you have put into finding the rights holder for an item you wish to digitize, you may come up against roadblocks. For instance, you might run into the situation where you cannot determine who the copyright owner of a work is, or the copyright owner never responds to your permission requests. The copyright owner may also decline to give you permission, or will charge you an unreasonable fee to use the item.[40]

In the case of the latter, if you still wish to use the item in a digitization project, you may wish to scale down your desired use of it (e.g., limiting use to the network in your physical location, or not putting the entire item online). From there you may be able to negotiate with the rights holder so that you can secure permission to use the item at a more reasonable price. Some rights holders will negotiate and others will not. If you still cannot get permission, you may need to substitute another item for it or not use the item in your project.[41]

ORPHAN WORKS

In the case of being unable to locate a rights holder, or the rights holder has not responded to your queries, you have happened upon what is known as an "orphan work." This means that the item is still under copyright, but the rights holders cannot be found. This is an issue that has hounded libraries and memory institutions for years; Congress and the U.S. Copyright Office have made attempts to study the issue and to create legislation, but none so far has been passed.[42]

When confronted with orphan works in a collection that you would like to digitize, you do have some options. If you initially conducted a fair use analysis on the work, you may wish to revisit it. If a rights holder was not found for the work then there may not be a large harm to the market for the item. A new fair use analysis may be different from the previous one based on the fact that you are dealing with an orphan work.[43]

It is also important to consult resources about orphan works to get a sense of best practices when it comes to including these materials in your library. There are two documents written by and for librarians and archivists that can provide such guidance on using orphan works: the Society of American Archivists' *Orphan Works: Statement of Best Practices* (2009) and the UC Berkeley and American University's *Statement of Best Practices in Fair Use of Collections Containing Orphan Works for Libraries, Archives, and Other Memory Institutions* (2014).[44] The *Orphan Works* best practices statement outlines "reasonable efforts" in detail to find rights holders of unpublished works; but its authors clearly state the usefulness of their document to locating rights holders of published works as well. It contains very detailed information on locating rights holders through collective licensing organizations, professional author organizations, and publishers. Additionally, this document contains a detailed bibliography of other sources to consult with respect to using orphan works.[45]

The *Statement of Best Practices* applies fair use to orphan works, and gives guidance on the following aspects of such collections: "1. Acquisition, 2. Clearances, 3. Selective Exclusions from Access, 4. Curation, 5. Conditions on Availability, 6. Dialogue with the Public, 7. Providing Copies to Members of the Public."[46] The "Acquisitions" portion describes the importance of donor agreements and appropriate description of rights within metadata. Upon acquiring a collection that may be digitized by your library, it is important to reach an agreement with a donor to have permission to make it available and to digitize it.[47] The "Clearances" portion covers seeking permission from a rights holder and the importance of documenting such a search.[48] "Selective Exclusions from Access" discusses the importance of potentially needing to exclude some works for reasons of protecting personal privacy as well as "third-party" materials that are likely copyrighted by others.[49] "Conditions on Availability" covers the basics of user policies with respect to orphan works in a digitized collection.[50] "Dialogue with the Public" states the importance of why a particular orphan work is made available as well as the prominent availability of a way for users to provide feedback on items in the collection.

This is a good faith measure that provides a channel for a rights holder to come forward and claim an orphan work. Such a means of communication for a potential rights holder to contact the library about an orphan work does not necessarily mean that the library will immediately remove the item from a digital collection.[51] "Providing Copies to Members of the Public" discusses the importance of making users aware of the fact that the orphan work they wish to use may still be covered under copyright and that they should not infringe copyright with their uses.[52]

END-USER POLICIES

End-user policies are also important to establish since they communicate important information on how patrons should use your digitized collection. They address copyright information on the contents of the collection, notifying users of their legal responsibilities in using works, and the ethics of how to properly cite digitized materials. To see a few examples, have a look at the "Legal" and "The Cabinet of American Illustration: Rights and Restrictions Information" pages of the Library of Congress.[53] The "Legal" page addresses the legal user policies for all collections such as copyright and privacy and publicity rights, as well as user privacy when using the site. The "Cabinet of American Illustration: Rights and Restrictions Information" page is specific to its respective digital collection. It briefly describes what is in the collection, reproduction permissions, publication in outside sources, as well as how to cite an item from the collection.

Here are some examples of sample language from the Georgetown County Public Library, Flora Public Library, and the Banning District Library:

1. **Images from the Georgetown County Public Library (South Carolina):** The link at the end of the following quote will show you a "Rights" field in the description. "The images in this collection are part of a private collection. All rights are reserved and the images may not be reproduced. For more information, contact the Georgetown Library at 405 Cleland Street, Georgetown SC 29440. (www.gcdigital .org/cdm/compoundobject/collection/p15077coll18/id/26/rec/1)."

2. **Here is some language from the Flora Public Library in Illinois:** "Charles and Katie Overstreet have generously allowed the Flora Public Library to borrow their collection for digitization. To order reproductions or inquire about permissions, contact Flora Public Library, 216 North Main Street, Flora, IL, 62839-1510 (618-662-6553). Please cite

item title and collection name." To see this used in the description of an item please see: www.idaillinois.org/cdm/compoundobject/collection/fpl/id/350/rec/1.

3. **The Banning District Library has a digitized collection of historical local photographs. Here is the end-user policy language that they use in the description of an item:** "Copyright status unknown. Some materials in these collections may be protected by the U.S. Copyright Law (Title 17, U.S.C.). In addition, the reproduction of some materials may be restricted by terms of gift or purchase agreements, donor restrictions, privacy and publicity rights, licensing and trademarks. Transmission or reproduction of materials protected by copyright beyond that allowed by fair use requires the written permission of the copyright owners. Works not in the public domain cannot be commercially exploited without permission of the copyright owner. Responsibility for any use rests exclusively with the user." Here is a link to an example: www.oac.cdlib.org/ark:/13030/c8pz59hq/?brand=oac4.

WHAT DO I DO IF I RECEIVE A COPYRIGHT COMPLAINT?

This is probably the most frequently asked question regarding placing digitized materials on a library's website. What does the library do if it receives a take-down notice or other complaint from an alleged copyright owner? Both the *Statement of Best Practices in Fair Use of Orphan Works for Libraries and Archives* along with the *Code of Best Practices in Fair Use for Academic and Research Libraries* address only part of this question. Both advocate for an obvious communication channel for copyright owners to register an objection to placing their work online.[54] The *Orphan Works* statement goes slightly further to state that an institution should not immediately take down the offending material, but should keep communicating with the copyright owner in question.[55]

CASE STUDY ■ ■ ◥ ————————————————————————————

DUE DILIGENCES AT THE SAN FRANCISCO PUBLIC LIBRARY

The Daniel E. Koshland San Francisco History Center began in 1964 as the California Collection at the San Francisco Public Library (SFPL).[56] The collection of primary and secondary sources on the history of the city is located in the Main Library building. The SFPL has 27 branches and in 2013–2014 had well over six million total visits and a budget of $96.9 million.[57] When the history collection started acquiring material the pieces were not logged and paperwork documenting donation or acquisition was inconsistent. This changed in 1996 when the library gained a city archivist who implemented changes to maintain records for new materials. The History Center currently has over two million photographs and provides access to digitized versions, which has required some research into the copyright status of some items.

Who Owns the Copyright?

Christina Moretta, photo curator at the San Francisco History Center, has experience with determining copyright status. When looking at the photograph collection for possible images to include in the library's digital collection, Moretta looks for materials which are obviously in the public domain due to age. For materials which may be under copyright she searches for any donor information which transferred rights to the library. This could be a letter, donation form, or notes made by a previous librarian. If there is no paperwork associated she looks to the image for clues; a building which can be used to date the photograph, the mark of a studio, or notes on the image such as names or dates.

From studio information she can check business directories to determine the business timeline and owners. With a name she can search on Ancestry .com for possible heirs. She will contact individuals and start corresponding with these people to document the materials and gain permission to place them online. This effort can take days or weeks. Moretta tries to emulate the efforts of a researcher and spends a reasonable amount of time to determine if the work is an orphan. Throughout this process she keeps a record of her efforts which show her findings and prove there was an attempt to locate any copyright holders. If there are concerns regarding a piece, the library is able to consult the city attorney for advice. In the case of a collection of videos from a local broadcasting station, Moretta has set those items aside until she has completed her research, including consulting experts at other archives to trace who may still have the rights.

When an owner is found and permission is given to place the image online, a note is added to the metadata regarding rights. The library uses different terms depending on who holds the copyright. If rights are held by the photographer, this states "Restrictions Apply" with the name of the photographer. For materials where the rights holder is unknown or is in the public domain, "Restrictions May Apply" with the name of the collection. Some images instruct those interested in using an image to obtain permission from the library.

Audio/Visual Rights

Knowing the rights status of a film is required when nominating a work to the California Audio Visual Preservation Project (CAVPP). This project, hosted by University of California Berkeley and made available on the Internet Archive, digitizes and preserves audiovisual materials from Californian libraries. This program was very tempting for the SFPL, which wants to preserve its collection but does not have the refrigerated storage needed to protect old film.

Determining copyright for audiovisual materials can be difficult without the equipment to view the material, or without the ability to see the images without damaging fragile film. Among the materials from the SFPL that have been digitized by CAVPP are several films of San Francisco's 34th mayor George Christopher, which were given to the library by his family. The library had the documentation transferring rights to the library. Another film, *Giant Trees of California,* was an Edison film produced in 1912 and was in the public domain due to the age of the film. One film canister had a label simply stating "parade." This piece, which is a little over one minute in duration, was found, after digitization, to be of President Franklin D. Roosevelt's first visit to San Francisco in 1938. Unlike the Edison film, it was past the 1923 date and did not include any information about the creator such as a title segment. This item could still be covered by copyright but could also be an orphaned work. The library felt that the likelihood of the original creator of the film still being alive was minimal and if someone stepped forward regarding the piece it could be taken down from the site and the history behind the film could be more fully documented. This position could be expressed in the rights statement.

CAVPP requires all audio/visual materials to include a rights statement and libraries are able to choose from a selection of these that best describe the situation. For the Roosevelt film this states "Copyright status unknown ... San Francisco Public Library attempted to find rights owners without success but is eager to hear from them so that we may obtain permission, if needed. Upon request to info@sfpl.org digitized works can be removed from public view if there are rights issues that need to be resolved."[58] This is a basic statement which can be included for any material for which copyright cannot be determined.

Moretta estimates the amount of time between a nominated film being accepted and placed online is about eleven months. This provides additional time to research and determine the copyright status. For some of these materials the preservation of the film trumps that of access, and there are some materials which were not sent to CAVPP which the library has digitized with other funds in order to safeguard the content.

Copyright Holders

When the copyright status is in question the boilerplate statement asks that the library be contacted. This happens very rarely. In one case a photographer saw one of his images in a book and contacted the author, who informed him that the image was at the library. In this instance the issue was that the photo was not attributed to the artist. This person did not mind having the photo online but did want credit for the work and the library was happy to oblige. In another case a woman had given the images to the library but objected to those items being online. The library took those images down and maintains the originals.

In cases where there is a copyright challenge Moretta will communicate with the individual and explain how and why the materials are available online. If the person is not satisfied the state archivist may join the conversation, and if necessary the city attorney's office can be consulted. The library always has the option of removing a digital item from the collection. These occurrences are very rare, and even if there is an issue the library can keep the digital files and has the possibility of gaining important information about what was once considered an orphaned work.

The SFPL has chosen a policy of making materials available with the knowledge that it might be asked to remove access. To minimize the possibility of this occurring the library starts with materials known to be in the public domain or with rights transferred to the library. When copyright is in question the efforts to determine the owner are documented. Your library should determine what will work best for your situation and workflow.

Chapter Synopsis

This chapter was not meant to be a comprehensive resource in copyright law as it applies to digital collections in any library. It was meant to serve as an introduction to copyright matters that a public librarian may need to know from the beginning of a project. Please be sure to consult the resources cited to gain further knowledge of this topic. To summarize, here are the main points to consider from this chapter:

- Copyright subsists in a work from the moment of its creation. No registration is needed.
- Copyright owners have the exclusive rights to copy, make derivative works, distribute, and publicly perform or display their works. In the case of sound recordings, copyright owners also have the right to digitally transmit such work.

- The creator of a copyrighted work is the one who usually owns the rights to it. However, these rights can be transferred—in whole or in part—to others.
- Donor agreements ensure that the library has the right to digitize the items and to make them available in the manner that they would like. They also help to clarify whether the donor owns the copyright to items in their donation.
- Copyright in the U.S. typically lasts for the life of the author plus seventy years. Works published before 1923 are in the public domain. Unpublished works created prior to 1895 are in the public domain. No sound recording will enter the public domain until 2067.
- Fair use allows for uses of copyrighted works for purposes of teaching, criticism, research, or comment. In an infringement case, a judge will analyze the use against the following four factors to determine whether the use was fair:

    - *Purpose* of the use.
    - *Nature* of the copyrighted work (fiction/highly creative versus nonfiction/factual).
    - *Amount* of the copyrighted work used.
    - The *effect* of your use on the market for the copyrighted work.

Tools such as Kenneth Crews's *Fair Use Checklist* and codes of best practices in fair use can assist you in making a determination on whether your use might be fair.

- It might be necessary to get permission to use a copyrighted work in your digitization project. Start with the work you'd like to digitize for clues on who may be the rights holder. Also search the U.S. Copyright Office's databases as well as other rights holder organizations.
- In some cases, it may not be possible to locate a rights holder even though the work is still in copyright. These are called orphan works. Librarians and archivists have created statements of best practices on this issue with respect to documenting search efforts to find the rights holder as well as the legalities involved in using orphan works.
- End-user policies help your patrons to understand how they can and cannot use digitized works in your collections.

NOTES

1. "Copyright and Other Restrictions That Apply to Publication/Distribution of Images: Assessing the Risk of Using a P&P Image," Library of Congress website.

2. Tammy Ravas, the author of this chapter, is not a lawyer and cannot provide legal advice. This chapter is written with the intent to provide authoritative information on the matters of copyright and digitizing collections in public libraries. None of it should be taken as legal advice. Please consult a licensed attorney, preferably one with a specialization in copyright law, should you need legal advice.

3. Statute of Anne; April 10, 1710, Yale Law School, Lillian Goldman Law Library website, http://avalon.law.yale.edu/18th_century/anne_1710.asp.

4. U.S. Constitution, art. I, sec. 8, cl. 8.

5. Subject matter of copyright: in general, 17 U.S.C. §102 (a).

6. Ibid.

7. Remedies for infringement: Damages and profits, 17 U.S.C. § 504 (c).

8. *Capitol Records, Inc. v. Thomas-Rasset,* 692 F. 3d 899 (8th Cir. 2012).

9. Exclusive rights in copyrighted work, 17 U.S.C. § 106.

10. Limitations on exclusive rights: Reproduction for blind or other people with disabilities, 17 U.S.C. Sec. 107-121.

11. Kenneth D. Crews, *Copyright Law for Librarians and Educators: Creative Strategies and Practical Solutions,* 3rd ed. (Chicago: American Library Association, 2012), 31–38.

12. David Ensign, "Copyright Corner: Copyright of Photographs," *Kentucky Libraries* 76, no. 1 (Winter 2012): 27–28.

13. Laura Gasaway, "Questions and Answers—Copyright Column," *Against the Grain* 19, no. 1 (February 2007): 57; Caroline Daniels, "Providing Online Access to Oral Histories: A Case Study," *OCLC Systems & Services* 25, no. 3 (2009): 176–77.

14. Dwayne Buttler, "Music and Copyright" in *Copyright Law for Librarians and Educators*, 3rd ed. Chicago: (American Library Association 2012), 112.

15. Eric Harbeson, *Ownership in Institutional Sound Recordings* (Helsinki, Finland: World Library and Information Congress, 78th IFLA General Conference and Assembly, 2012), 9–12, http://conference.ifla.org/past-wlic/2012/148-harbeson-en.pdf.

16. Buttler, "Music and Copyright" 112.

17. Carrie Russel, *Complete Copyright for K-12 Librarians and Educators* (Chicago: American Library Association, 2012), 108–09.

18. "A Guide to Deeds of Gift," Society of American Archivists website, www2.archivists.org/publications/brochures/deeds-of-gift.

19. "A Guide to Deeds of Gift."

20. Curt Witcher, personal interview with the author, August 20, 2014.

21. Ibid.

22. Duration of copyright: Works created on or after January 1, 1978, 17 U.S.C. § 302 (1976).

23. Ibid. (c).

24. Ibid. (c), (e).

25. Ibid. "Hirtle, P. (2010). Copyright Term and the Public Domain in the United States. Retrieved from http://copyright.cornell.edu/resources/publicdomain.cfm.

26. Hirtle, P., Copyright Term and the Public Domain in the United States.

27. Ibid.

28. Limitations of exclusive rights: Fair use, 17 U.S.C. § 107 (1976).

29. Ibid.

30. U.S. Copyright Office, *Circular 21,* pp. 6–8.

31. Pat Aufderheide and Peter Jaszi, *Reclaiming Fair Use: How to Put Balance Back into Copyright* (Chicago: University of Chicago Press, 2011), 94–107.

32. Ibid., 108–26.

33. *Code of Best Practices in Fair Use for Academic and Research Libraries* (Washington, DC: Association of Research Libraries, 2012), 19.

34. Ibid., 20–21.

35. Crews, *Copyright Law for Librarians and Educators*, 56.

36. Limitations on exclusive rights: Reproduction by libraries, 17 U.S.C. § 108 (1976).

37. Crews, *Copyright Law for Librarians and Educators*, 139–41; Rebecca P. Butler, *Copyright for Teachers and Librarians in the 21st Century* (New York: Neal-Schumann, 2011), 29–31.

38. Crews, *Copyright Law for Librarians and Educators,* 142.

39. Butler, *Copyright for Teachers and Librarians in the 21st Century*, 33.

40. Crews, *Copyright Law for Librarians and Educators,* 143.

41. Ibid.

42. *Report on Orphan Works* (Washington, DC: U.S Copyright Office, 2006), http://copyright.gov/orphan/orphan-report-full.pdf; Shawn Bentley Orphan Works Act of 2008, 110th Congress, S.2913 (2007–2008).

43. Crews, *Copyright Law for Librarians and Educators,* 143.

44. *Orphan Works: Statement of Best Practices* (Chicago: Society of American Archivists, 2009), www2.archivists.org/sites/all/files/OrphanWorks-June2009.pdf.; *Statement of Best Practices in Fair Use of Collections Containing Orphan Works for Libraries, Archives, and Other Memory Institutions* (Berkeley: University of California Press, 2014), www.cmsimpact.org/fair-use/best-practices/statement-best-practices-fair-use-orphan-works-libraries-archives#twentynine.

45. *Orphan Works: Statement of Best Practices*, 2–11.

46. *Statement of Best Practices in Fair Use of Collections Containing Orphan Works for Libraries, Archives, and Other Memory Institutions*, 27.

47. Ibid., 28.

48. Ibid., 30–31.

49. Ibid., 32–33.

50. Ibid., 35.

51. Ibid., 36.

52. Ibid., 37.

53. "Legal," Library of Congress website, www.loc.gov/legal/; "Cabinet of American Illustration: Rights and Restrictions Information," Library of Congress website, www.loc.gov/rr/print/res/111_cai.html.

54. *Code of Best Practices in Fair Use for Academic and Research Libraries*, 20; University of California Berkeley and American University, 36.

55. *Statement of Best Practices in Fair Use of Collections Containing Orphan Works for Libraries, Archives, and Other Memory Institutions*, 36.

56. "About the San Francisco History Center," San Francisco Public Library website, http://sfpl.org/index.php?pg=2000019101.

57. *San Francisco Public Library Annual Report: By the Numbers, 2013–2014* (San Francisco: San Francisco Public Library), http://sfpl.org/pdf/about/administration/statistics-reports/annualreport2013_2014.pdf.

58. "President Franklin Delano Roosevelt in San Francisco," Internet Archive, https://archive.org/details/csf_00002.

CHAPTER 3

OVERCOMING STAFFING LIMITATIONS

I think the most important thing if you're interested in doing this is being sure that you have other people from the start to help support you.

—Patricia Johnson, director, Stewartville Public Library, Minnesota

You work on the reference desk all day. How do you have time to start something like a digitization project? There are few people who work in libraries who have time to spare. How do you take on an additional project when you already are working the reference desk, fund raising, planning events, and tackling the many other projects that end up in your list of duties? How can you add more without breaking the camel's back?

COLLABORATION AND PARTNERSHIPS

Does your library have the staff and equipment to create digital versions of your important collections? Staffing, expertise, and equipment need not remain barriers to creating digital collections. Collaborations and partnerships can help make digital projects possible. There are already many examples of cooperation among libraries, from interlibrary loan agreements that make a world of information available to shared catalogs that reveal the combined collections within a system, state, and beyond. The tradition of cooperation among libraries naturally extends to digital projects.

Libraries all over America have found partners whose expertise, resources, and shared knowledge make digitization projects successful. Universities, state libraries, historical societies, and local institutions are often willing to scan, provide metadata for, and host digital items for libraries that have interesting collections but may not have all the resources needed to present a searchable collection to the public. These partnerships can supplement your library's expertise, staff, and funding to make your collections widely available online.

State libraries have often taken the lead in these types of cooperative arrangements. An Institute of Museum and Library Services survey found that State Library Administrative Agency (SLAA) "funded or facilitated digitization or digital programs and services for different users, including" 40 state libraries, 16 other state agencies, and 31 libraries or library cooperatives.[1] These programs typically offer a combination of training, scanning, metadata, and hosting services. Federal funding in the form of IMLS and Library Services and Technology Act (LSTA) grants distributed by these agencies are a couple of the main sources for funding digital projects.

The Power of Partnerships

Having the support of like-minded institutions can be vital for making your digital dreams a reality. One partnership which resulted in a successful collection was between the Nebraska Library Commission and the Fairmont Public Library. Wanda Marget, director of the Fairmont Public Library, was able to develop a collection while working part time as the library director, taking care of the local cemetery, maintaining the town website, and editing a monthly newspaper. Fairmont is a town of 600 located 60 miles southwest of Lincoln, Nebraska. When the Nebraska Library Commission began offering grants that would provide her with the opportunity to create a digital collection, Marget accepted the funds. Digitization was completed by the Nebraska Library Commission, which sent an individual to the library to scan images. The library remained responsible for the metadata. In some cases Marget relied on her knowledge of the community to locate individuals who could provide details for the history of the images. One photograph of the telephone office led her to four women who had worked for the telephone companies. The resulting metadata from this effort is a short history of the telephone and telegraph offices in the town. All four women in the photograph were named, the telephone office identified, and the rivalry between the different companies, the locations of those offices, and company mergers are described.

When the project was completed there were almost fifty images available in the digital collection. Images ranged from an aerial photograph of the city to an interior view of Mrs. Tony's Café. Because Marget was able to work with the Nebraska Library Commission, the only aspect of the digitization process she needed to complete was the metadata, and in that effort she was aided by community members.

This example of one person's efforts leading to a wonderful digital collection was made possible due to a number of factors. The library was able to get a grant through a state-level agency and that agency provided digitization services. The library did not have to host the materials which are available on the site: Nebraska Memories. This type of collaboration paired with grant opportunities can be vital to getting your library's collections online.

DIGITIZATION

Digitization, or scanning, is one of the first steps in creating a digital collection. Depending on the equipment used, the type of image, the fidelity of the scan, and the number of items in a collection, it can be a long and sometimes tedious process. The cost of scanners and scanning services has dropped in recent years, but the time required to scan a whole collection may not be feasible for some libraries.

Prices will vary depending on the type, size, and number of items to be digitized. There are businesses and organizations which offer a variety of options for digitization projects. There may be an organization, such as a digitization hub, in your state that can provide support. If your library would like to establish a more formal arrangement with an institution that can assist with one or more phases of the creation of a digital collection, investigate opportunities to partner with either a larger public library or a local university. In many states larger libraries and universities have developed digital collections programs aimed specifically at assisting smaller public libraries and other local institutions with digital projects.

Supporting Regional Libraries

In Ohio the state library has provided LSTA grants combined with funds from the Ohio Public Library Information Network for four public libraries to purchase equipment necessary to become digitization hubs. These regional hubs, which include the Columbus Metropolitan Library, Cleveland Public Library, Public Library of Cincinnati and Hamilton County, and the Toledo-Lucas

County Public Library, will work with historical societies, libraries, museums, and other institutions to scan collections, provide metadata, and host materials. Hosted collections may eventually be included in the Digital Public Library of America. By taking on all aspects of digitization projects, from digitization to metadata to hosting, these hubs help ensure consistency and quality within and across the digital collections they create. Offering this level of support will require more work for the hubs but will help them meet the need for high-quality scanning and consistent metadata.

The Columbus Metropolitan Library (CML) is one of the libraries that has taken on this role. It provides assistance with planning, scanning, rights management, and metadata. Angela Oneal, manager of local history and genealogy at the CML, is in charge of developing these services. The digitization efforts at CML date back to 1998 when the library started with small-scale projects. The library hosted its own collection until a collaboration in 2006 with the Columbus Historical Society led to the creation of Columbus Memory. The new equipment and funds that resulted from this partnership allowed the library to increase its digitization efforts and create sub-collections such as one focused on African Americans, which contains newspapers, photos, and pamphlets.

When the opportunity arose for the library to join other Ohio public libraries becoming digitization hubs, the CML had the staff and experience not only to be a leader, but to be an active resource for other libraries. Transitioning to a hub was a natural evolution in the library's services. According to Oneal, "the hubs project offered us an opportunity to institutionalize a regional approach and offer some services beyond what we were already doing at our library." The grant provided funding for new equipment, allowing the library to provide improved services. The library already takes advantage of a shared licensing agreement for hosting materials, but the new equipment will be central to facilitating the digitizing of collections as well. The change in services, the acquisition of new digitization equipment, and the influx of a larger variety of material formats and sizes in other institutions' collections has required a close evaluation of workflow and changes in the way the library handles different projects.

As a hub the CML supports other institutions at a number of different levels. It provides training that includes how to plan a digital project, the goals for the collection, and how those goals will impact the project. For example, if a library is creating a digital collection to accompany an anniversary celebration where access and timeliness are the main considerations, the training may not include in-depth information about digitizing for preservation. Participants will be walked through the planning process, and CML staff will work with the library to determine how it can be supported and the plan completed. Training is offered for those willing to learn the digitization processes of scanning and adding metadata.

The CML has reevaluated collection selection, prioritization, digitization, and metadata. Previously the library was able to prioritize digital projects based on patron needs and the historical significance of collection materials. Now the CML accepts projects that meet the library's selection criteria of material relating to central Ohio. With the selection criteria in mind, the staff look for items of unique historical importance with a connection to the region. Copyright, technical considerations, and whether the owning library can handle some aspects of the digitization process are also considered. If a library cannot help with metadata or scanning and the material falls within its collection requirements, the CML will consider taking on the whole project in order to preserve and increase access to those materials. The CML is working to digitize as much as possible while stretching budgets and staff.

To streamline the process each item received will be accompanied by an intake form recording descriptive information necessary for metadata entry. The information provided may go beyond Dublin Core requirements by including detailed descriptions which read like short histories. A photograph titled "Charles Grossman and Theresa F. Grossman" provides detailed information on the couple, their clothing, when they immigrated to the United States, how many children they had, and some history regarding the photographer.[2] An image from 1969 of a sign reading "Free X-Ray Today" was loaned by the Breathing Association and provides a short history of that organization's efforts to prevent and control tuberculosis.[3]

The physical intake form stays with the materials throughout the process. The document is sometimes completed by having a staff member sit down with the owner and fill out the form. When working with an institution rather than an individual from the community, training sessions on how to fill out the forms are offered if needed. If an institution cannot provide anyone to become familiar with the forms, materials or doesn't have the staff available to enter detailed information, the basic information is provided and CML staff will fill in the remainder of the metadata. Forms submitted are double-checked by CML staff who work with the donor to help them determine if the material is really theirs (family photos) or if they own copies of someone else's work. To avoid managing rights for the many personal collections, the library will not provide high-resolution copies of materials loaned by private individuals. When working with other libraries there is a Memorandum of Understanding

(MOU) between the libraries explaining how the CML will handle the digital collection. A rights statement is included in the object description: "A user of any image in this collection is solely responsible for determining any rights or restrictions associated with the use, obtaining permission from the rights holder when required, and paying fees necessary for a proposed use." This statement leads the users back to the source library.

The intention of the CML is that the library, historical society, or other institution will become actively engaged in the process and that the contributing institution's strengths will be utilized. Although the library is willing to perform all aspects of the digitization process, contributions in the form of metadata, digital files, and other resources are welcomed. The library wants to develop a hybrid model where it offers "a little bit of everything depending on what resources the partner brings to the table." If the contributing institution has digital files and metadata, the CML will upload the material into the Columbus Memory project. This will help the library take on more projects by supplementing library staff, allowing the CML to assist more libraries.

HOSTING

Are you ready to host your own collection? Hosting requires space, maintenance of files, and an access point. Not all libraries will have the means to maintain digital collection platforms and files and may instead seek to partner with a hosting institution. State libraries, universities, and historical associations have been developing consortium agreements to pool resources and to offer centralized online locations for state collections. Public libraries, academic libraries, museums, and historical associations can then contribute collections to a single, digital collection platform, resulting in a large collection comprised of smaller holdings. Members may become digitization hubs, but more commonly these groups serve as content holders, providing access to diverse digital collections related to a state or region.

Building Conglomerate Collections

You don't have to have a single large organization like a state library or a university to generate the resources to support digital collections. There are many cooperative organizations which have combined their resources and developed conglomerate collections. The New York Heritage Digital Collections hosts the collections of over 200 New York institutions with content ranging from images to letters and photographs.[4] The Galway Public Library brought together a collection of ten historic images of Galway from the Galway preservation society and from community members. Some of these images subsequently made their way into *Reflections of Galway*, a Galway Public Library and Galway Central School Collaborative book and website. The Bethlehem Public Library has contributed forty-four photos, letters, and legal documents to the New York Heritage Digital Collections. The Clifton Park-Halfmoon Public Library has contributed over 500 items, including a letter from 1855 complaining about a highway worker who never appeared for work, photos of Depression-era amusement park concessionaries, sepia-toned images of the construction of a reservoir, and family photos documenting generations of local families. The many collections, large and small, are available via an online digital collections platform containing hundreds of thousands of items. Distinct pages provide information about each contributing institution and where original documents are located.

New York Heritage is a project of the NY 3Rs Association that brings together regional digital collections from nine councils, including Central New York Heritage, Western New York Legacy, Capital District Library Council Digital Collections, Long Island Memories, North Country Digital History, and others. When collections are brought together there are benefits for the public as well as for the participating libraries. Researchers spend less time locating and searching a large number of collections. The collections are easier to find and instruction for use is simplified because the aggregated collections can be searched in the same way. It is also easier for users to remember the location of a single resource rather than locations for many diverse collections. The aggregating hubs also take responsibility for keeping the materials available.

If your library is interested in digitizing but unsure about how to provide and maintain a digital collections platform, collaboration with a hub or collaborative collection may be a good solution. Contact your regional or state collaborative group to learn about contributor requirements, guidelines, and to find out if they are accepting new content. The Library of Congress's *State Digital Resources: Memory Projects, Online Encyclopedias, Historical & Cultural Materials Collections* lists digital collections initiatives for all fifty states plus twelve multi-state collections. Your state's memory project may offer grants or be willing to assist with digitization, metadata, and hosting services for your collection.

COLLECTION-SPECIFIC SUPPORT

There may be support for your library based on the type of material you are digitizing. StoryCorps, a nonprofit, started in 2003 and has worked to record over 50,000 interviews, 45,000 of which are housed with the American Folklife

Center at the Library of Congress.[5] A portion of these recordings are broadcast on National Public Radio and are available online or through partners. A 2014 pilot study with the American Library Association (StoryCorps @ your library) resulted in ten libraries receiving support in the form of training and online tools. This program will continue in 2015 with another ten libraries selected to participate.

The Nashville Public Library participated and "chose to specifically record and preserve the oral narratives of the city's Latino, Somali, Laotian, Kurdish, Vietnamese, Sudanese, first-generation and other foreign-born, immigrant, diverse communities."[6] The library partnered with Lipscomb University, specifically with Professor Richard Goode's United States History course. Students registered family, friends, and community members for the project and conducted interviews. This was the second time students from Professor Goode's class had assisted the library. Previous students had collected interviews for a collection focused on first-person accounts of a devastating 2010 flood.

The Nashville Public Library also collected oral histories and documents from 400 veterans. This was in response to a call for partners from the Library of Congress (LOC). Support from the LOC was primarily in the form of "partner packets" with instructions on how to conduct the interviews, collect materials, and complete forms. If the library had a question it could call the LOC and receive assistance from a staff member. The library found the overall experience to be good.

Small segments of some of these interviews are available on the library's website. These snippets of narratives range from under a minute to three minutes and provide an example of the types of stories told. The samples were kept short due to the amount of server space available, to make the audio clips user-friendly, reduce the length of transcripts required for each piece, and to focus on interesting stories appropriate for a diverse audience. One consideration was that the stories shared were of war experiences, which could be graphic and not appropriate for young students and some content might be edited out from the sample.

According to the special collections division manager, Andrea Blackman, The Flood 2010 NS Storycorps @ Your Library projects led to the Nashville Public Library working with ten new community partners. With the Flood project partners included the mayor's office, the Matthew Walker Comprehensive Health Center, McGruder Family Resource Center, and the YMCA Fifty Forward. With the Storycorps project the library worked with Conexion Americas, Casa de la Cultura, the Center for Refugees and Immigrants of

Tennessee, Lipscomb University, Brentwood Library, Belmont University, and the Mayor's Office of New Americans.

The stories presented online are primarily from World War II veterans. When the collection was first made accessible online the program had only recently started interviewing veterans from Vietnam, but the material available encourages the curious to dig deeper into the collection. The library's participation in the Veterans History Project ended in 2012. The congressionally mandated program has, with the help of numerous partners, collected over 68,000 interviews.[7] More than 7,000 of those are available online at the Veterans History Project website.[8]

Newspapers

Newspapers offer wonderful insights into the past, but the volume of the material might make a digitized collection seem infeasible. Hosting for such large collections is also a challenge. Chronicling America provides a single source for multiple collections of newspapers. The service is the product of a partnership between the Library of Congress and the National Endowment for the Humanities (NEH) and has its origins in the United States Newspaper Project, which started in 1980 and ended in 2007. That project sought to locate and preserve American newspapers and resulted in a "bibliographic description of over 140,000 newspaper titles and the creation of close to one million local holding records."[9] This project created an index of library holdings which, while not complete, served as a powerful research tool and source of data for the eventual digitization project. The National Digital Newspaper Project (NDNP) started in 2003 to "provide permanent access to a national digital resource of newspaper bibliographic information and historic newspapers, selected and digitized by NEH-funded institutions (awardees) from all U.S. states and territories."[10] Like other initiatives, this project draws from large collections and cooperative digitization efforts such as the Oregon Digital Newspaper Project.

Current expectations for the NDNP program include digitization from microfilm holdings and newspapers that were published before 1923. This cutoff date is to limit holdings to public-domain materials. As of August 8, 2014, there were 8 million newspaper pages available from thirty-seven states, one territory, and the District of Columbia. South Dakota and Nevada are two of the more recent additions to a program which is "encouraging interoperability and providing the tools to make it possible to have produced many instances of collaboration that have widened each institution's coverage, expanded the content of their holdings, and provided a support network."[11] Eighty percent of the cultural institutions contributing to the North Dakota collection have collaborated with other organizations, and 65 percent have partnerships outside of the state. One of the benefits of this program is that the partnering institute is often the repository of master microfilm copies of newspapers. This allows libraries to focus on the grant writing necessary to pay for digitization while the rest of the work is performed by the partner working with its own microfilm. The distribution of work takes the full burden off of a single library.

WORKING WITH A VENDOR

If your state does not have a digitization hub or other partnership opportunities there are a number of for-profit companies which provide digitization services. The benefits of outsourcing scanning include not spending limited funds on equipment, having items professionally scanned, and saving the efforts of library staff and volunteers. Although someone will still need to inventory, pack, and ship materials to the vendor and to review the quality of the digital files provided by the vendor, in-house digitization requires in-house expertise and equipment that may not be available.

If you are considering outsourcing scanning, metadata, or hosting, check other libraries' collections. When you find an example that you like, contact the library and ask about the vendors they used. Ask if they would recommend the vendor or if they have any suggestions about how to make the experience of working with a vendor as productive as possible. By asking colleagues or using electronic discussion lists you can limit yourself to companies that have experience with libraries and obtain the opinions of trusted individuals. There are organizations that collect information on vendors, such as the Association for Information and Image Management, which maintains a directory of companies.

Before contacting a vendor, know the size, number, format, and any special requirements for the materials to be digitized. If there are fragile materials that need special handling, you will need to know how the vendor will digitize them without damaging the originals. How do you expect your users to interact with the collection? Will you need to have materials undergo OCR (optical character recognition) scans searchable by specific categories, or accessible for individuals with disabilities? You will need to decide what types of files you will want and how they will be made available. Confirm with the vendor that it can provide the file types you want and can deliver them on the hardware that you specify.

Ana Krahmer of Northern Texas University Libraries reminds librarians in Texas to make sure that the vendors they use will create files that will meet the quality standards required for inclusion in the National Digital Newspaper Project. She has seen cases where a vendor promised a level of quality that it could not provide. Not all vendors will offer the same service or provide the same level of results.

Outsourcing Large Collections

Senior Special Collections Librarian Jeremy Drouin of the Kansas City Public Library in Missouri says his library has outsourced the majority of its digitization projects and has "used a variety of vendors, just depending on what is to be scanned." Individual vendors have been found to work with oversized materials, fragile items, and other formats. Large-format materials are best scanned using equipment that has been designed to accommodate those sizes. Fragile, bound materials require a book scanner that supports the binding, and these types of scanners are more expensive than a good flatbed, desktop scanner. The library will digitize a small number of items in-house but will outsource the scanning if the collection contains a large number of items. Many of the library's collections contain large numbers of items, with 650 advertising cards, 432 images in the Askren Photograph Collection, 605 assorted photographs, 1,200 autochrome photos, 318 biographies, and 23 other collections focused on regional history.

Librarian Craig Scott from the Gadsden Public Library in Alabama realized that with their level of staffing they could not spare anyone to scan their collection of photographs. Instead they contacted a company in Provo, Utah. This company sent a staff member with two scanners. Instead of sending the collection of irreplaceable photos across the country the library reserved a space for the woman who would scan the materials. For two full weeks, from eight in the morning till eight at night, she digitized all 4,500 images. Before the woman arrived the library staff had already started working on the metadata, which was entered into Excel spreadsheets. This arrangement offered several benefits. The material stayed in the library, library resources were not used, and staff could focus on metadata creation. Because the person who was scanning the images brought her own scanning equipment, regular library activities were not interrupted. Scott was relieved that library equipment would not be "disconnected and moved into the conference room and disrupt our own operation here while they brought everything, they brought their own scanners, the equipment." After the scanning was complete the company matched the metadata to the images at its site in Utah.

For the Gadsden Public Library, using a professional company saved staff training time, met their quality requirements, and was generally a good experience. As with any vendor, experiences can vary, but there are steps your library can take to ensure desired results.

- Find information about the history of the company, the size of its staff, and the age and type of equipment they use.
- If you are sending material to a vendor, learn how the transportation will be handled, how your materials will be stored, and if there is any security.
- Ask for a detailed quote on the cost including the per-image cost, shipping, and data transfer.
- Make sure the vendor understands the "project scope, details, and output specifications, and confirm that the vendor can support them."[12]
- Ask for a sample based on your material.
- Ask the vendor for a list of references, and contact them.
- Clarify expectations, including the amount of time needed for completion. This will help to ensure that your library's expectations are met.

VOLUNTEERS

Volunteers can be a considerable force within a library. In 2012 it was the volunteers who were used as a reason to prevent the privatization of the public library in Oceanside, California.[13] In many libraries volunteers are necessary to meet the day-to-day needs of the library. According to a 2006 IMLS study, "among the public libraries that have digitization activities, 17.2 percent train current staff to perform digitization activities and 9.1 percent use volunteers."[14] Volunteers already fill many of the library's needs, and digitization is another area where a volunteer can contribute. With training and support, your volunteers can take charge of entering metadata, scanning, and website maintenance.

Large institutions have been using volunteers to help process and add metadata to their digital collections. In 2010 the Australian Museum used volunteers to scan and enter short records for 16,000 insect specimens.[15] Smaller institutions can rely on volunteers for digital projects such as the Chelsea District Library in Michigan, where a librarian with almost fifty volunteers digitized 15,000 records from a family history index.[16] The collection consisted of 4 × 6 inch index cards on which obituaries were pasted. This popular local history index took two years to complete, from October 2005 to October 2007. The public can now search a database of names and locate citations or obituaries for families.

Strategies for Successful Volunteers

The Allen County Public Library in Fort Wayne, Indiana has two important strategies for success in dealing with volunteers, one of which is to have a volunteer coordinator who works in recruitment for the whole library system. When a volunteer is needed, this coordinator is contacted. The coordinator then reaches out to the local historical associations and genealogical societies as well as to other organizations for interested volunteers. The support in the community is strong enough that up to 100 volunteers can be mobilized at once.

The second strategy for the success of the volunteer program is the way the library treats the individuals who donate their time. Volunteers are trained and supported like other staff members. Staff work with them to determine their areas of interest and any training needs, and then matches them with a project they will find rewarding. Each project is explained in terms of both the needs of the job and the importance of the material. High-interest items such as World War II letters, photographs, and materials with local meaning are offered. Volunteers are valued, mentored, trained, complimented, and encouraged the same way as the library's paid employees are. Individuals start slowly and receive regular training, feedback on their work, and correction when needed. This method of training at the beginning of a project ensures that volunteers know the correct procedures, develop confidence in their skills, and have a high quality of work. By working closely with the volunteers at the start of a project, the comfort level and the interest of a volunteer can also be evaluated to make sure the project will be a good fit or to find other options if the work is not right for that person.

The primary work phases of a digital project include scanning, metadata creation, and uploading metadata and digital files to a digital collections management system. The volunteer is asked what they would like to do but are not required to perform only one task. They can switch to different work if scanning or metadata entry becomes too monotonous. This flexibility helps to prevent burnout and keeps volunteers interested in their work. Once a volunteer is trained they may be moved from one project to another if a need arises. When a local church disbanded and approached the library about scanning its historic documents, there was a time limit; the library would only have the church's materials for thirty-one days. Because of this deadline some volunteers were shifted from different projects and others were called in to scan the materials. In this instance the focus was on scanning as many documents as possible. Little metadata was entered with the expectation that the information would be added later.

An Amazing Volunteer: It Only Takes One

The Allen County Public Library's Genealogy Center has one volunteer who has made a highly significant contribution to the library's digital collections. In a perfect pairing of interest and knowledge, this volunteer has single-handedly scanned and provided metadata for a collection of over 9,800 images. Librarian Curt Witcher found a super volunteer, "a retired firefighter who just happened to be a professional photographer as well." This gentleman offered his own collection of photographs as well as the collection at the local fire museum. The volunteer, Donald Weber, had a large personal collection with images of parades, anniversaries, fire houses demolished and opened, fund-raisers, and burning homes; this personal collection was further augmented with older materials through Weber's connection with the local firefighters and the fire fighter museum. The Clay School fire of 1894 shows a three-story building wrapped in smoke. The 1947 Cilppinger Studio fire shows wet, dark-suited men climbing a ladder to a window as thick, billowing smoke pours over them. There are photos of school children attending educational programs in the 1950s alongside color photos of fashion shows from 1975. Due to Weber's knowledge of the fire department, the equipment, and the town, he has been able to pro-vide detailed descriptions of events from ladder training to traffic accidents.

Entering metadata into the content management system was not something with which Weber was originally comfortable. A self-described Luddite, he was not initially interested in working with the available data-entry technology. The library does what it can to match the available technology with the comfort levels of the volunteers, so an Excel spreadsheet was set up for his use, which could then be uploaded into the system. Eventually, Weber was open to trying the system again and became proficient with the software. According to Witcher, over fifteen years Weber "has personally scanned and keyed the metadata because he knows all the material. He either took the picture or worked with the fire museum." This one volunteer has scanned and provided metadata for over 9,800 fire-related photographs. Weber may jokingly refer to himself as an "old man" or claim that "I don't do that computer stuff," but the collection he has created is a testament to his dedication and his skills. Thanks to his efforts the community he cares about is well represented in the library's collections.

Witcher is proud of the library volunteers and understands the value of these dedicated individuals. The library staff work with the volunteers to find areas of interest which will make their jobs interesting and rewarding. Sometimes these matches are obvious. In the case of Weber, he had an interest in sharing his collection and having the work he has devoted much of his life to repre-sented in the library's collection. The library's dedication to the volunteers is reflected in the way the volunteers take their work and the library very seriously.

Witcher feels that volunteers are worth the investment of time and training in them. He understands that some libraries may perceive "volunteers as people who can do something useful but they take a lot of time and it's just not worth the trouble," but his experience at the Allen County Public Library has shown him the value in treating these core library supporters like library staff. The time investment has paid off and produced thousands of images now in the Allen County Community Album, a testament to their efforts.

Student Volunteers

Students receiving internship credits by working at a library can be wonderful, dedicated workers. Palin Bree at the Boyce-Ditto Public Library in Mineral Wells, Texas, had a high school student who "would plug in her MP3 player and scan for a couple of hours each week." This individual followed the parameters required by the University of North Texas Libraries' Digital Projects Unit, and produced consistently good work. The student scanned the majority of the first items in the library's collection but eventually left for medical school.

Losing volunteers is to be expected. Mona Vance-Ali, archivist of the Columbus–Lowndes Public Library in Columbus, Mississippi, often uses students from a local college. The students have focused on scanning, which stops once the student graduates or has finished an internship. A volunteer may be active for four months or several years. They may complete a project or leave before it is done. Although losing a volunteer requires finding a replacement and providing additional training, they remain a valuable resource.

Vance-Ali tries to find one college intern per semester and often draws from the History Department of the local college to find individuals who will be interested in the content and might have some knowledge of the time in which the material was created. She will often have three interns a year. While Vance-Ali understands the value of her volunteers, sometimes it is good to take a break from training and working with interns to focus on other projects "because while it's fantastic to have both volunteers and interns they do require time for me to manage them." By using student volunteers Ms. Vance-Ali has the flexibility to focus on digitization or other tasks as needed. When she requires assistance for scanning or other aspects of digitization, she knows she can look to the high schools or the local colleges for volunteers.

THE DRAWBACKS OF VOLUNTEERS

Volunteers are often transitory and this is accepted. Students will move on, retirees will have other interests, and community members will have other obligations. Some volunteers will not be suited to a task or may vanish without notice. When these individuals leave, your project may stall until a replacement can be found and trained. If the volunteer was in charge of the website or database, finding someone with experience with your software could be a challenge. The collection at the Billings Public Library in Montana started with "the systems administrator and a volunteer and they scanned everything in and uploaded and it was about 115 items and very little metadata and then it sat there for a few years. Then I [Kathy Robins] got involved with it, it ended up being me and an intern who were involved so again it was just two people." There is a limited amount of work one staff member and an intern can accomplish.

The success of your volunteers will be based on finding the right volunteer for the job, and providing training, support, and oversight. Expect to take the time to train and check the work of your volunteers. Vance-Ali found that "there's going to be human error but the quality of the volunteer or intern really is imperative." It is always better to perform quality control and guidance early in a project than to have to go back and fix or redo a large amount of work.

CASE STUDY

THE POWER OF VOLUNTEERS

According to *A Brief History of Madison* (New Hampshire) the community was originally part of another town called Eaton, which was named in 1764 after General John Eaton.[17] Madison was created as a separate entity in 1852. A main feature of the community is Silver Lake, described in 1925 as a place where "one may lie in a boat and gaze into summer skies fringed with majestic mountains, and for the time be beguiled into thinking he is in fairyland."[18] The lake, where poet E. E. Cummings had a summer home, still attracts many summer tourists, as do a number of impressive features such as the largest known glacier-deposited boulder of granite.[19]

Before 1995 the library was housed in what had been a one-room schoolhouse. Private donations led to the building of the current library, a two-story, white, cape-style structure. Library collections, the children's area, two work tables, four computers, and the reference desk are on the second floor, which is about 2,000 square feet. The first floor has a meeting room which can accommodate forty people. Madison has a population of around 2,500 and a library budget of $76,136.[20]

The digitization projects at the Madison Public Library prove that you do not need an army of volunteers to have great digital collections. Much of the scanning and metadata work has been completed by five volunteers.

Current projects have at least five volunteers: one person who scans, two people dedicated to transcribing vital statistics, and two people transcribing town newspaper columns. Because Madison attracts people who enjoy the lake in the summer and skiing in the winter, the volunteers change with the seasons, but the library normally has around five volunteers at any given time, allowing for consistent progress on the projects. Former library director Mary Cronin understands that these individuals are valuable and a highly sought local resource. The library has limited staff and the community members who volunteer their time "are also volunteering at about ten other things. There's only so much so many people can do." Being in a small town with a population that fluctuates with the seasons is a challenge for the library, which is competing with other local institutions for volunteers.

The library uses various methods to find volunteers, but the most effective tool has been the library newsletter. According to Cronin, her most successful method of finding volunteers includes calls in the library newsletter with descriptions of current projects and promises of training. When a potential volunteer contacts the library, Cronin would learn the person's interests, skills, and what type of training they would be willing to complete. She then would match that person with a project. Recently this has led to a volunteer with good technical skills offering to edit audio files from oral history interviews. Another tool for finding volunteers is the library's web page for the digital collections. An open solicitation for items of local historic interest is posted with links to digitized materials.

There is a consistent source of people with time and interest in local history. When looking for volunteers, Cronin often looks for individuals who have recently retired, are open to learning new skills, and "have a lot of energy." Often these volunteers come with skill sets and experience with different technologies. One of the skills many volunteers have is typing. The modern keyboard is based on a configuration that is over 100 years old.[21] If your volunteers were born after 1890 there is a good chance they have used a keyboard before and can enter metadata. These individuals are also familiar with handwritten documents, which is an important skill for creating transcripts.

One of the successful strategies employed by the Madison Library involves the way volunteers are trained. All volunteers will benefit from training, and at the Madison Library each worker gets personal attention. Cronin, in part due to the size of the library, notes that "everything we do is one-on-one as far as training goes"; this includes learning what skills the person has, what they are interested in learning, and matching them to a project. This personal, hands-on approach allows Cronin to find that area of interest that results in volunteers who enjoy the work and are less likely to burn out on a project. The limited number of people working on the projects leads to a strong sense of ownership among the volunteers, who see the progress for which they are responsible.

The library tries to identify and utilize the strengths that each volunteer brings but also wants any prospective volunteer to understand that they do not need to be experts in any field. Working personally with each volunteer will help them to gain the skills they need and make them feel like a valuable member of the team. As they learn new skills they feel pride in their accomplishments and are mentally stimulated. The work is engaging, there is flexibility within the projects, and the importance of their efforts is apparent. Furthermore, being a small library is a strength when working with volunteers because they will know the staff and have a clear perspective on how their work is contributing to the mission of the library and how their efforts make the project possible.

The library also employs several strategies for retaining volunteers, including recognition. Volunteers receive recognition for their work in each metadata record that is created. Records include the names of the person who scanned the image or created the transcript. The rewards of volunteering are often nebulous and depend on the individual—if they feel pride in helping others, if they enjoy learning more about their community or learning new skills. Including the names of the people who are spending their time to type transcripts, scan documents, and input metadata is a simple way to say thank you. Linking the person to the project is also a way to remember various volunteers who can point to the records as one of their accomplishments. When community members see how the library values the efforts of their volunteers, they themselves may be more inclined to join the library's efforts.

The materials that the volunteers work with are varied and help volunteers maintain interest in the work, which can be repetitive. Cronin has found that "once they start working on them they get kind of fascinated with them, even the vital statistics." The vital statistic requires the entry of names and dates which could be dull work if not for the fact that the volunteers see the births and deaths of individuals belonging to the same family over a long period of time and engage with the histories. The wide assortment of materials has another goal. Having a variety of items—oral histories, maps, photographs, and transcripts—provides examples of the types of materials the library is interested in digitizing and encourages the lending of materials and inspires people to volunteer.

There are three main projects currently in process: town columns, vital records, and town reports. Town columns are original manuscripts of news columns written in the 1970s and 1980s. These pieces of contemporary history appeared in the local newspaper and describe local events. The original, handwritten manuscripts were donated to the library, which is now working on transcriptions. These short pieces were compiled because they are interesting, and volunteers working on this project enjoy reading these snippets of local history.

The vital records project has been directed by Bobbi Slossar at the New Hampshire State Library, who has trained librarians around the state to create searchable databases that can be combined into a larger collection. Vital records in Madison were first recorded in the nineteenth century when towns were required to provide birth and death information to the state of Maine. The result is a searchable database available on the library website which will eventually be linked to a state-wide database of historical vital records. While working on this project, volunteers noticed that some early records had birth and death records entered at the same time. This occurred frequently for individuals born before birth certificates were common. This was a surprise for the volunteers who, according to Cronin, noticed "especially in the 1920s and 1930s the people who never had a birth recorded." Birth certificates were issued retroactively when the person died. This information provides insight into how birth records were kept, and entering this information into a database will aid genealogists. The library has transcribed the statistics up to the 1930s. According to Slossar, the transcripts can take between several months and a year to complete.

The town reports also have a long history, with the first report published in 1893. For this project, the library has some external assistance. The library is scanning the reports, which will be hosted by the University of New Hampshire. The university library has been collecting these documents from around the state and is adding them to the library's collection. In this case Madison is helping the university library by providing the files for a collection to which the university is actively adding. These reports give detailed accounts of the town's finances and expenditures. Reports from the school district and other agencies are sometimes included and provide details about items such as salaries and the costs of books and heating stoves. The process for getting these reports digitized and online has been slow since the university is working on uploading reports for the whole state, but Madison has been able to help by scanning its documents to the university's specifications. Community members are entering the metadata for the reports.

Volunteering Documents

The Madison Library accepts items from local community members for inclusion in its digital collections. When library patrons bring material to the library to be added to the digital collections, the library staff collect information about individuals and dates but keep the process simple to encourage the sharing of these items. The materials that are coming to the library are the result of Cronin's call to the community for "any kind of history, local history items that might work with our history archive." This includes materials salvaged by sharp-eyed individuals when homes are cleaned out for sale. The library scans the material and returns the original to the owner. Donor information is included in the metadata which is displayed with the digital version.

One distant user found the library's online collection, which led to the library obtaining original copies of founding documents the owner's family had possessed for generations. The people who lend their personal treasures are also acknowledged in the notes in the metadata record, where the information they have provided lends insight to the personalities of the people in the photos. One photograph of Lucy (Phillips) Nickerson contains information from a report by a family member: "If you look closely, you'll notice Lucy is wearing a set of [rose gold] beads around her neck. Joshua gave them to her when they were married; they were passed down through the generations, and I now have them."[22] This type of information provides another level of interest, turning the portrait of an elderly woman into someone with direct and current ties to the community.

The library still has one project that needs an interested community member—the oral history project which is part of the Library of Congress's American Folkways Center Veterans History Project. The library has a digital recorder and instructions for people to record conversations. The local veterans associations have been approached, but as of this writing the library is still looking for a community member who is interested in capturing the stories of the community. Despite general acknowledgment in the community that these oral histories are important and should be collected, no one has stepped forward to help.

The lack of volunteers had not been due to a lack of effort on the library's part. Cronin has tried to involve the local veterans association in the hope that "vets might be more comfortable speaking to other vets but even that didn't pan out, not yet anyway." Not all efforts to recruit volunteers will be met with automatic success. The Madison Library will continue its efforts to find a community member who understands the value of oral histories. It may take time to locate the right person for the job, but it may only take one passionate individual to take this project from start to finish. ■■■

Chapter Synopsis

Libraries of all sizes are creating wonderful digital collections despite the challenge of staffing. The ways in which these projects are accomplished are as diverse as the libraries themselves. Of the libraries interviewed, those who were creating some of the most impressive collections had certain characteristics in common.

- **Collaboration:** Very few of the libraries interviewed for this book tried to create or host a collection by themselves. Find other institutions or agencies that can help you meet your goals.
- **Volunteers:** These dedicated individuals are important participants in the creation of digital collections. Of the 30 libraries interviewed, 11 used volunteers to help them reach their goal.
- **Using volunteers:** Most volunteers help with scanning and metadata but a few are helping with the library website and databases.
- **Finding volunteers:** Historical societies and schools are good places to find volunteers.
- **Matching interests:** The most successful projects have volunteers who have worked with staff to match their interests to the projects. A volunteer who is interested in the subject matter is more likely to stay with the project, but cross-training can help to prevent burnout.
- **Training volunteers:** Treating your volunteers like employees can provide structure and help the volunteer feel like part of the library team.
- **Outsourcing:** You do not have to do all the work yourself. If you have funding, outsourcing may be an option.

All these resources, volunteers, digitization and hosting hubs, and partnerships make the creation of digital collections feasible for even the smallest libraries. Many libraries have also found that by working with others they can preserve and increase access to important library collections. You can, too.

NOTES

1. D. W. Swan, J. Grimes, K. Miller, and L. Bauer, *State Library Administrative Agencies Survey: Fiscal Year 2012* (Washington, DC: Institute of Museum and Library Services, 2014), 19, www.imls.gov/assets/1/AssetManager/2012%20SLAA%20 Report.pdf.
2. John A. Pfeifer, *Charles Grossman and Theresa F. Grossman*, 1881–1890, photograph, Columbus Metropolitan Library, http://digital-collections.columbuslibrary.org/ cdm/compoundobject/collection/memory/id/19833/rec/210.

3. *Free Chest X-Rays Available within X-Ray Cruiser, 1969*, 1969, photograph, Columbus Metropolitan Library, http://digital-collections.columbuslibrary.org/cdm/compoundobject/collection/memory/id/28185/rec/227.

4. "About," New York Heritage Digital Collections website, http://newyorkheritage.org/about.

5. "About Us," StoryCorps, http://storycorps.org/about.

6. Janel Shoun-Smith, "Students Join StoryCorps to Preserve History of Nashville's Immigrants," Lipscomb University website, February 26, 2014, www.lipscomb.edu/news/archive/detail/13/27890.

7. Veterans' Oral History Project Act, Pub. L. No. 106-380 114 Stat. 1447 (2000), www.gpo.gov/fdsys/pkg/PLAW-106publ380/pdf/PLAW-106publ380.pdf.

8. "Veterans History Project," Library of Congress website, www.loc.gov/vets/vets-home.html.

9. Mark Sweeney, "The National Digital Newspaper Program: Building on a Firm Foundation," *Serials Review* 33, no. 3 (2007): 188–89.

10. "About the Program," Library of Congress website, www.loc.gov/ndnp/about.html.

11. "Award Recipients," Library of Congress website, www.loc.gov/ndnp/awards/.

12. Jamie Mears, *National Digital Newspaper Program (Impact Study 2004–2014)* (Washington, DC: National Endowment for the Humanities, 2014), 7.

13. Marisa Ramirez, "Going Digital: Questions to Ask When Outsourcing Digitization," *MLA News* 50, no. 1 (2010): 21.

14. Allison St. John, "Oceanside Public Libraries Not Up for Bid." *KPBS*, www.kpbs.org/news/2012/mar/16/oceanside-public-libraries-not-bid/.

15. "Status of Technology and Digitization in the Nation's Museums and Libraries," (Washington, DC: Institute of Museum and Library Services, 2006), www.imls.gov/assets/1/AssetManager/Technology_Digitization.pdf.

16. Paul Flemons and Penny Berents, "Image Based Digitisation of Entomology Collections: Leveraging Volunteers to Increase Digitization Capacity," *ZooKeys* 209 (2012): 203–17, doi:10.3897/zookeys.209.3146.

17. Public Schools of Madison, *A Brief History of Madison* (Madison, NH: Madison and School Library, 1925–26), www.madisonlibrary-nh.org/madisonhistory/wp-content/uploads/2012/05/brfhist_madison.pdf.

18. Ibid., 3.

19. "Madison Boulder Natural Area," Parks & Recreation New Hampshire website, www.nhstateparks.org/explore/state-parks/madison-boulder-natural-area.aspx.

20. Strategic Planning Committee and Board of Trustees, *Madison Library: Strategic Plan 2015–2017* (Madison, NH: Madison Library, 2014), http://madisonlibrary-nh.org/WP/wp-content/uploads/2013/12/Strategic-Plan-final-10.17.14.pdf.

21. Stan J. Liebowitz and Stephen E. Margolis, "The Fable of the Keys," *Journal of Law & Economics* 30, no. 1 (1990): 33.

22. *Lucy (Phillips) Nickerson*, Madison Library Local History Project website, www.madisonlibrary-nh.org/madisonhistory/2013/03/03/lucy-phillips-nickerson.

CHAPTER 4

GETTING YOUR COMMUNITY INVOLVED

Libraries are changing so we've pretty much been in the forefront of making community connections and really trying to take library services and programs outside the library walls and to the community.

—Melissa G. Lane, manager of local history and digital preservation,
Gail Borden Public Library, Illinois.

Your library is a very special institution. Libraries are perceived as safe places that support the community and are a source of trusted information.[1] Libraries are places where values like culture, freedom of information, freedom of access to technology, the importance of literacy, and preservation of the past are shared by many users. Many people in your community believe in the mission of your library and are willing to vote for taxes to support your organization. A 2010 OCLC study found that respondents felt "libraries provide the personnel, technology, information resources and physical environment that meet their needs."[2] Statistical studies before and during the Great Recession (2007–2009) found more people turning to the library for resources and assistance than in non-recession years, and a 2012 report from the IMLS found a 20.7 percent increase in library visits over ten years.[3] The library is a place people seek out for reliable resources in good times and bad. As a result there is often a high level of trust and loyalty among library users.

A strong relationship with the community is further solidified when that community is asked for assistance or advice. Reaching out will show your patrons that you value their opinions, stories, and talents. Asking for advice can increase empathy, strengthen bonds with community members, and provides an opportunity to reach traditionally underserved populations.[4] One way of encouraging community involvement is through a volunteer program, but this is often limited to a few individuals who are able to regularly work at the library. There are other ways to reach larger numbers of people by asking for content, going to their location, or using technology to make connections between user interests and library needs.

COMMUNITY METADATA: DRAWING ON LOCAL MEMORIES

When Emily Meloche of the Chelsea District Library in Michigan needed help identifying individuals within a large collection of photographic negatives, she knew where to look for assistance. A local photographer had retired and given the library boxes and bags of negatives which after processing resulted in forty-eight linear feet of material. Some envelopes had handwritten names with varying degrees of legibility and others had little information regarding the people in the photos. Meloche called the local senior center and asked if any of the residents would assist her with identifying any of the individuals in the photos. Meloche hoped a few of the area seniors might be willing to help identify the events and people, but the response was even greater than expected. When she arrived that first day there were twelve seniors waiting. This regular event has become very popular, generating excitement over the collection while helping the library create accurate metadata to accompany the images. To prepare for the sessions Meloche has the scanned images on PowerPoint slides, numbers the slides and the individuals pictured, and includes any information that came with the images. During the sessions the attendees review the photographs and accompanying information in the projected slides and offer corrections and identifications of individuals. Minor errors are caught early and corrected to improve the accuracy of the metadata.

With this system the seniors are also able to solicit more information from friends or acquaintances who may pore over old yearbooks on their own to identify people in the photographs. If the group cannot name everyone in the image it is common for someone to volunteer to gather more information by seeking out others. Meloche found that participants may say, "Well, I don't know everyone in this photo, but I'm getting lunch with the groom in this wedding tomorrow, so let me bring him a picture." In addition to these instances of inspired recruitment of friends beyond the regular meeting time, there are dedicated individuals who wish to include friends unable to attend the meetings. These individuals are provided copies of the images to show to those who aren't able to come to the senior center. This program of working with the seniors once a month has significantly helped with the creation of metadata for the collection.

Meloche estimates that one third to one half of all individuals in the photographs have been identified. Although this is a good rate, the volunteers have higher standards and are frustrated if the identification rate is less than 100 percent. The seniors of Chelsea are up to the challenge and look forward to the monthly event as an opportunity to socialize and reminisce. The photographs are the focus of conversation and when people in the projected images are recognized, stories are shared about the specific individuals and events. The stories are part of the overall experience, and time and space are taken to allow these narratives and conversations to happen. Although the goal is to collect metadata, the events are very social, a time to share memories and connect with others.

One of the reasons this regular event is so popular is because the volunteers enjoy what they are working on even if they may have started as unwilling participants. One woman who became a regular attendee was first brought, reluctantly, by a friend. She was quiet as others chimed in to identify people, and although she probably did know some of the people in the photos she was not the first to speak. This changed after about twenty minutes when a pre-wedding photo of a woman in her bridal dress lit the screen and she recognized herself. When the slides came to the woman's wedding pictures Meloche was happy to see "she was able to identify every single person in them." After this session she was eager to attend the regular event and now volunteers to scan images.

As a result of the popularity of this event, three individuals have also volunteered to help scan the negatives to provide content for the identification session and prevent cancellation due to a lack of images. The volunteers have already shown their dedication and neither rain, sleet, nor hail will keep them from the monthly event. When the meeting was scheduled on a particularly snowy day it was canceled, much to the disappointment of the participants. Meloche was concerned that the seniors "were going to go out there, dig their cars out of the snow and ice to get there to identify photos. I had to say 'No, stay home, we'll all stay home today.'" These regular meetings are meaningful to the participants, who enjoy the opportunity to socialize and provide valuable information. The meetings give them a unique volunteer opportunity to share their knowledge, experience, personal memories, and time. Because they enjoy these meetings they are willing to reach out to a larger network of friends and acquaintances.

The Chelsea Public Library is able to have such successful involvement from its community members because they feel their contributions are valued by the library and they are adding to a resource of considerable significance. Their voices are adding to the historic record of the community. Your local senior center or other groups may also be interested in lending their expertise to your projects.

COMPILING HISTORIES, PRESERVING PERSPECTIVES

Libraries and librarians often see one of their roles as that of protectors of local history. Their users also recognize this and bring materials to the library to be saved and preserved because libraries are seen as an obvious partner with a shared interest in local culture and history. Carolyn Tremblay, reference librarian at the Dover Public Library in New Hampshire, feels "it's important to save as much of Dover's history as possible." Mona Vance-Ali of Columbus-Lowndes Public Library prefers to keep original materials for long-term preservation. One of the reasons the Flora Public Library wanted Charles Overstreet's photos was because it felt the materials needed to be preserved, and for Craig Scott in Gadsden the primary reason to digitize is "preservation and the second reason, an important reason, would be public access." Many of the librarians interviewed felt they needed to collect and preserve local history because the library was the only local institution with both the interest and the means to safeguard and provide access.

Access to material given to the library is a concern of researchers. Alexander Maxwell, senior lecturer at the School of History, Philosophy, Political Science & International Relations at the University of Victoria at Wellington, wrote of digital archives: "I only care about improved access."[5] There is an expectation that these historic materials will be available in the library's collection, if not online. But what happens to that perception of that history if something is missing?

Accurate Reflection of the Community

Some libraries such as the New York Public Library have reputations for serving a diverse population with equally diverse collections with over 100 years' worth of non-English newspapers and documents. Not all libraries have had the funds, space, expertise, or support to collect materials in multiple languages or from all of a community's populations. As you look at your collections with an eye towards digitization, ask yourself: does your collection accurately reflect your community?

The history of your collection, the outreach efforts of the past, and the way your library has been perceived by the community can all have a significant impact on the materials obtained through donations or solicitations. Taking a good look at the history of your library and location may reveal some omissions. Many librarians currently embrace a philosophy of inclusion, where the library is open to anyone who seeks to use the books, computers, the space, or who needs information. This was not always historically true of every library or the policies dictated by the values of the community. Some libraries have always been open to all while others were open to a select group of patrons.

This has even been true of the American Library Association. In 1936 when the ALA held its annual conference in Richmond, Virginia, members were upset that the events were segregated, with African American librarians unable to eat in the same room or stay in the same hotel. Members were told that this was to conform to Virginian laws. LeRoy Charles Merritt wrote to *Library Journal* that "under no circumstances should the A.L.A. allow Negro discrimination to occur at any library conference."[6] His thoughts were similar to others who wrote that the conference should never have taken place under such conditions.

The American Library Association's *Library Bill of Rights* states: "A person's right to use a library should not be denied or abridged because of origin, age, background, or views." The first *Library Bill of Rights* was written in 1939 and was influenced by censorship and the spread of fascism in Europe. Full of good intentions, the statement supported librarians but was useless against Jim Crow laws and segregation. Even if a librarian believed in equality, the desires of the empowered segment of the community could make sure the library was a place of exclusion by firing librarians and replacing them with someone who would uphold the current societal norms. This was the case in 1950 when Ruth Brown was dismissed from the Bartlesville Public Library in Oklahoma for fighting to integrate the library. Many libraries, especially in the South, excluded non-white populations while others had underfunded branch libraries for African American communities.[7] There were, however, many exceptions. By 1953 "59 Southern cities and counties permitted 'full use' of the main public library to African Americans." After the Brown v. Board of Education decision in 1954 more libraries desegregated. In 1966 the U.S. Supreme Court, in a case where a group of African American were arrested for peacefully protesting the segregation of the public library, ruled that the "regulation of libraries and other public facilities must be reasonable and nondiscriminatory and may not be used as a pretext for punishing those who exercise their constitutional rights."[8]

Given the historic situation, it is not surprising that in some places people who felt excluded may not have trusted the library to hold their family records and documents even when efforts were made in the past to cultivate a more inclusive public space and collection. This results in historic collections that document a predominantly white history and present a one-sided historical perspective. This is an issue that is larger than just library collections. One example of how this can affect the perception of a community is described by Martha Menchaca, who found that in the community of Santa Paula in California the story of the non-Anglo founders and residence was absent from the library archives, the city museum, and government plaques. The omission of these individuals from the local history

> produces a distorted history. . . . Indeed, these historical gaps are a problem, as the contributions and accomplishments of Mexican origin people and Native Americans are attributed to Anglo Americans. Furthermore, by not including within Santa Paula's historical records accounts of the marginalization and discrimination suffered by Mexican origin people, those who chronicled Santa Paula's past relegated such happenings to insignificance.[9]

How do you reach out to a community that is underrepresented in the library's holdings? If members of a community have been discriminated against in the past or present, they may be hesitant to share their personal treasures with a local library. When local history librarian Bill Bell of the Banning Library District in southern California received training as part of his LSTA grant from California, it included analyzing collection materials through the lens of representation. He realized "we had like zero from our black community in Banning, very, very few of the Mexican-American community, none of the Hmong community which has been a large population." The collection of photographs from the Native American community was also limited. Despite the fact that the community was and is diverse "99 percent of the photos were of white people so that was a problem." Recognizing the gap in the collection, Bell actively sought to add materials to the collection from these groups.

When you ask your community to share their personal photos and documents you are telling the community that you value their experience and history. You are saying that their history is important to you and worthy of preservation. Asking to share their materials as opposed to donation is important because you are not asking them to give up material with personal significance. Before digitization this required individuals to trust the library to keep and preserve their materials while the individual lost easy access to what could be very personal photos, letters, and scrapbooks. This could limit what people were willing to share and result in collection gaps such as the ones the Banning District Library in California wanted to eliminate.

Banning is a community between two mountain ranges, with the San Gorgonio Mountains to the north and the San Jacinto Mountains south of the city, which is about 40 miles west of Palm Springs. The area was explored in 1855 as a possible route for the railroad to the Pacific reaching the then small port towns of Los Angeles and San Diego. A stagecoach line once passed through the arid area filled with groves of nut trees and native desert palms. The land had been claimed by the Spanish as part of the vast Mission San Gabriel Archangel lands and later as part of Rancho San Jacinto y San Gorgonio.[10] The area was already home to the Cahuilla tribe, who had lived in the area for hundreds of years.

The train did go through the pass bringing ranchers, homesteaders, outlaws, and others who would encroach on the Cahuilla lands. Later the dry, clean air and Mediterranean climate would draw people to sanitariums to treat tuberculosis. In the 1940s the first African Americans joined the community, which grew when land acquisitions by the city of Palm Springs in the late 1950s led to evictions and razed homes there. Many of the displaced people moved to Banning.[11]

The library was first established in 1916 and shared the same building as the school. In 1955 the library moved to a separate structure, but the administration of the library remained under the Banning Unified School District until 2005, when a bill passed by the Californian legislature granted a separate board for the library.[12] Banning now has a population of over 29,000 that includes Native American, African American, Hispanic, and Hmong residents, among other peoples.

If Banning had such a long history of cultural diversity, why was this not represented in the library's collections? When the Banning Public Library was established in 1916 it was closely associated with the school, and it is impossible to tell if librarians in the past felt archival materials were appropriate acquisitions for the collection or if Banning residents felt the library was the place to house their personal history. What really mattered now was that the current librarian was looking at the collection and finding that important segments of the community were not represented.

Rather than rely on the library's existing photo collection, Bell reached out to the community through a series of newspaper articles requesting people bring their photos and their stories to the library. They did, doubling the library's collection, but this was not easily done. Bell was frustrated with his initial efforts and wondered "Why aren't people sharing photos?" only to learn "a lot of it is because they didn't have them." Why did so many people in the community not have photographs? In a world of digital photography it is easy to forget that cameras were once less common and more costly.

Photography was once an expensive hobby. It wasn't until 1900 that Kodak introduced a camera that would change photography; the Brownie, a simple box camera introduced that year and advertised as costing one dollar. Loaded with film instead of glass plates, small and easy to use, the camera was highly popular. In 1905 the U.S. Census estimated the total population of the United States to be 83,822,000, and it is estimated that ten million Americans were amateur photographers.[13] Those who did have their picture taken before the popularization of the camera may have waited for special occasions such as weddings, family reunions, or other events. In later decades, when more people had access to cameras and collections of family photos, they may have not considered that their library would want or care for those materials.

The process of conducting outreach and acquiring additional photographs from underrepresented groups was a learning experience for Bell. Some people were hesitant to share these documents at all. His newspaper articles often requested more information from the community and illustrated that the library wanted to tell the story of the whole community. When people did bring their photos a scanner was used to digitize the original images, which were returned to their owners. As people viewed the images in the California Digital Archive and read the stories in the paper requesting information from the public, they were willing to bring their own photographs to the library to have them digitized and added to the collection. Perhaps even more importantly, those individuals who came to the library with images also came with stories which have been incorporated into the local history articles available on the library's website. Of the project Bell says there are always more materials, especially photographs, which then perpetuate the process when people see those images and recognize the library's interest.

The ability to digitize an item and return the original is a significant tool for adding to the library's collection. Bell has found this to be helpful "because you wouldn't want to give your family photos to an archive but, if you give them for a few months and they scan them and give them back that's a big plus." In working with members of the community Bell was also able to learn more about culturally sensitive issues. He had opportunities to learn some of the reasons behind the collection's lack of material relating to Native Americans. He found that for specific cultural reasons members of the local Native American community did not want to share their photographs with the library.

The Banning District Library has almost 400 images included in the Online Archive of California. Among photos of sweeping vistas, drying dates, and Chamber of Commerce brochures are images of students at the Indian School, Hmong children's choirs, early businesses and their owners, and diverse family photos. This collection shows the many faces of Banning and recognizes the contributions of these individuals.

Reaching out to the whole community provides opportunities for the library to develop more inclusive collections and document fascinating local history. For Bell this is just the beginning of a collection that will more accurately reflect the people of Banning and fill in gaps on the contributions of the Hmong, African American, and Mexican American communities. Bell feels the library's outreach efforts have "really opened some eyes to the town, really expressing who the town is or who the people are in the town, whereas prior to this I think a lot of these histories weren't acknowledged." By encouraging sharing instead of donation and actively working to tell the stories of the whole community, the library's collection is becoming more representative of the people who have called Banning home.

Reaching out to different communities can help you build a more representative collection. If you seek to include materials relating to Native Americans, there are protocols developed to facilitate these efforts. These have primarily been created for institutions that have cultural artifacts, but the advice could also be used for those seeking to present an honest representation of the community. One of the recommendations is to contact tribal officials and start a conversation. There is one content management system, Mukurtu, developed to provide flexibility for cultural materials. According to developer Kimberly Christian with the Center for Digital Scholarship and Curation and Washington State University, this system "makes it possible for indigenous communities themselves to manage those materials in ways that are culturally appropriate, and we are putting indigenous knowledge on the same level as that of the collecting institutions."[14] This system can provided different levels of access depending on the user and allows for more control over who can see specific collections. Mukurtu works with and is supported by the Sustainable Heritage Network, which provides workshops and tutorials focused on preserving cultural heritage.

An Organized Effort to Collect Neglected History

Even large libraries may have collections in need of diversity. The Los Angeles Public Library has a collection titled Shades of LA which focuses on oral histories and photographs from members of the community which reflect the ethnic diversity of the city. The collection was created when the librarians realized how little they had regarding the Watts neighborhood. The issue came to the attention of the library when researchers looking for images to mark the 25th anniversary of the 1965 riots in Watts found that the only image of the area in the library's collection was of the Pacific Electric railway station. As the library explored the issue it realized that it "owned few photographs from any of the ethnic communities that populated the city."[15] In a city as diverse as Los Angeles this omission of material was a significant issue.

Understanding the challenge of reaching a large and diverse public, the library sought help from organizations within the different communities. With the help of the Photo Friends of the L.A. Public Library, and historian and folklorist Amy Kitchener, the library shared its goal with these groups that then advocated for the project. The project was embraced by around 500 volunteers, including student interns from nearby colleges and universities. Over five years these volunteers worked with over 500 Los Angeles residents who shared their photographs.[16] To facilitate this level of interaction with the community there had to be procedures and training for the volunteers who would be working with the public.

Volunteers and staff used a guide which detailed how interactions would proceed and many of these were intended to show that the people and their materials were appreciated. Since the program was potentially looking at huge numbers of photographs, only a few could be selected from each individual. The guide included recommendations for the community members on the care of their old photo albums and suggestions for creating new books of memories. These include proper storage and identifying individuals in the images. This advice not only helps community members by giving good advice but also shows that the library cares about these materials even if they were not selected for inclusion in Shades of LA. Details for libraries on how to organize a photo day event range from fund-raising, the number of volunteers needed, equipment required, to refreshments and is intended to take a library through the whole process. The training guide reminds volunteers to use gloves to prevent fingerprints and to show the donors "we care about their photos and they will not be damaged."[17] The purpose of the project was to add to the library's collections, create a collection that accurately portrays the community, and help the community preserve its history.

The Los Angeles Public Library succeeded in collecting over two million photos through this initiative; these photos fill many of the previously discovered gaps in the collection and gives a more complete view of the history of the community.

CROWDSOURCING: COMMUNITY INVOLVEMENT THROUGH TECHNOLOGY

Crowdsourcing is a way to engage a community of interested individuals regardless of location. When used by cultural institutions it is similar to other efforts in which a library may already be engaging. The primary differences are in the reliance on technology to reach the community and the ability to have large numbers of volunteers. The possibilities for crowdsourcing in the United States are being explored by agencies like NASA and the Smithsonian Institute.

The term *crowdsourcing* can be applied to a number of activities but generally refers to an Internet-based collaborative opportunity.[18] Often there is an open call for people to contribute their personal knowledge or skills to the completion of a project. This can range from a call to the community to contribute photos of an event, create transcripts of letters, or add metadata to a document.

So why aren't more libraries taking advantage of this option? An important element of crowdsourcing is creating "a framework for participation" and this framework requires work, people who can manage the system, and funds to purchase software.[19] Software can range from free, open-source options to proprietary services costing several thousand dollars a year. With either option there will need to be some management of the system. The framework for participation can be a newspaper database where users register to correct OCR transcripts or a section for comments included in the metadata display. The results of this solicited work still need to be checked for accuracy.

In making these options available a user can be part of a large project with minimal effort. By announcing an open call for participants you are inviting users to interact with collections, improve searchability, add metadata, and contribute content. An easy-to-use access point enables users to contribute at their own comfort level.

Crowdsourcing does require software and management, but depending on your needs this could be minimal. Brian Geiger, director of the Center for Bibliographical Studies and Research (CBSR) at the University of California, Riverside, started a project to correct text in digitized newspapers. The software they used was originally created for the Australian Newspaper Digitization program. The CBSR was already using the vendor Veridian to host its newspaper collection, and for a modest increase in billing the library was able to add the OCR correction element.

Because this system is handled by a vendor the amount of additional work by the library is minimal, and Geiger estimates the amount of his time he spends on managing the system to be around 2 percent. Users have corrected about four million lines of text and the efforts are occasionally monitored for quality. Geiger has found the process to be surprisingly easy. An important aspect of the program has been the people who are taking time to correct the text and their level of accuracy. The OCR character accuracy for California Digital Newspaper Collection newspapers ranged from 70.4 to 92.6 percent. The corrected papers' accuracy ranged from 99.3 to 100 percent, with the greatest increase in a single paper (*Sausalito News*) changing from 70.4 to 100 percent word accuracy.[20] If the library had paid for this service, Zarndt and Gieger estimate the cost to be around $0.50 per 1,000 words or $11,560 for CDNC alone.[21] To hire someone to do the work would cost around $24,083.[22]

Can You Trust the Crowd?

Generally yes, you can trust the crowd. A number of studies have found that the efforts of diverse groups can have very accurate results. A number of large institutions including NASA and the Smithsonian Institute have trusted the masses with improving their digital content by inviting the public to assist with metadata. The National Library in Finland created a game to correct OCR scans of antique books, newspapers, magazines and journals. The project was highly popular with 55,000 individuals contributing with a 99 percent accuracy rate.[23] These institutions have found that the work produced is worth the effort and have found interesting ways to encourage participation.

What Motivates the Crowd?

Why do people spend their time helping libraries with crowdsourcing projects? Those who participate in these projects are people from your community and around the world who share common interests and enjoy sharing their knowledge. A study by Oded Nov found the majority of individuals in his survey of regular *Wikipedia* contributors were motivated by enjoyment of the work and the ideology behind the site.[24] Another study surveyed *Wikipedia* users at New York University and learned their motivations included educating others, a sense they were making a difference, and to give back to the *Wikipedia* community.[25] People often work on these projects to make their own research easier and to aid those with similar interests.

When the Library of Congress tried a pilot project where Flickr users could tag photos they learned how people were relating to the images through humor, emotion, and contributions of personal knowledge. A report on the project found that the library "appear(s) to have tapped into the Web community's altruistic substratum by asking people for help."[26] Of the 4,500 images placed online there were fewer than twenty-five comments which were humorous or inappropriate. Overall people liked being asked to contribute and took the responsibility of adding information seriously. The metadata added was primarily on locations, individuals, and sometimes links to articles and other resources.

The Cambridge Public Library in Massachusetts and the CDNC jointly surveyed the people who were assisting with a transcription project to learn more about the people who were taking the time to fix the pages of text. They found that most of the users considered themselves to be genealogists or family historians (67 percent CDNC, 76.6 percent Cambridge), the majority of user were between the ages of 50 and 70, and most transcribers were using the resources for family and local history research.[27] One user wrote that the information in the database matched with his personal interests in maritime history and that he was motivated to correct transcripts to make his own research easier and "to leave the corrected text for use of others."[28]

This altruistic perspective was a common theme among the transcribers who listed their motivation as a desire to aid others who are engaged in research. In 1998 Janine Nahapiet and Sumantra Ghoshal argued that "in order to contribute knowledge, individuals must think that their contribution to others will be worth the effort and that some new value will be created, with expectations of receiving some of that value for themselves."[29] Individuals who are correcting text may see not only their contribution as an effort to improve the searchability for others, but also themselves.

What Is the Crowd Good for?

You look into the night's sky and you need to identify possible locations of planets. Far beyond the recognized constellations are planetary nurseries that can be detected by infrared wavelengths. These have been captured in thousands of images taken by NASA's Wide-field Infrared Survey Explorer. How do you document all the possible needles in a haystack encompassing the cosmos? In a groundbreaking project, NASA invited the public, citizen scientists, to aid in this effort by personally checking the images for signs of debris disks and young stellar objects.

The Smithsonian Digital Volunteers Transcription Center has also sought public assistance in creating transcripts of journals, typed manuscripts and books, money, as well as labels from specimens of bumblebees. Their volunteers range from school children to experts, all of whom are contributing to the increased online availability of these materials. The New York Public Library has used crowdsourcing to provide full-text access to a collection of menus and to create a tool aligning historic maps to modern New York streets allowing users to see changes in the urban landscape.[30] There are some volunteers who have made significant contributions including "one user [who], for instance, single-handedly georectified nearly an entire Brooklyn street atlas, well over 200 sheets."[31]

Crowdsourcing has many potential benefits such as augmenting the number of workers on a project, reducing the amount of time needed for project completion, building online communities, engaging users to better understand their interests, building trust, and strengthening the connection with the community.

Improving Newspaper Searchability

For the Cambridge Public Library in Massachusetts crowdsourcing is transforming OCR errors in newspapers from an unintelligible jumble to a searchable text. Users are invited to register by filling out a simple form. Once this is complete the user can select articles to correct. As large amounts of newspaper text is corrected the people who perform the task are closely interacting with historic documents and connecting with local history.

The Cambridge Public Library's Historic Cambridge Newspaper Collection contains over 59,000 pages of historic newspapers, 40,000 subject cards, and 13,000 obituary cards. The transcription correction program, Veridian, divides the text into lines that can then be fixed.[32] The project has over 170 users who have corrected more than 230,000 lines of text. The project started in 2012 and the accuracy of the transcribers has made a significant impact on the searchability of the newspapers.

In 2014 the Cambridge Library performed a study on newspaper use in the library. They found that library patrons were using both the print and digital versions of the newspapers. Use of the Historic Cambridge Newspaper Collection (HCNC) was far greater than other digital newspaper collections, including the library's subscription to the Historic New York Times database. The HCNC collection had 11,209 sessions with 40,359 page views between April 1 and May 15, 2014. In the same time period the *New York Times* database had 803 sessions and 2,393 page views, and the *Boston Globe* had 1,161 sessions and 1,197 page views.[33] This high usage may be attributed to the Cambridge collection being the only free, searchable source for these public domain materials. According to a survey of the library's patrons, microfilm is still used when a digital version is not available. The *Cambridge Chronicle* years available online are 1846–1922 (public domain) and 2005 to the present through Newsbank, which library card holders can access from home. This leaves eighty-three years' worth of newspapers available only in microfilm. Even though it is not the most popular format "patrons continue to use it steadily and even slightly more than the online *Cambridge Chronicle* provided by NewsBank" and "print newspaper use has remained steady over the past 10 years, although patrons are accessing digital editions more and more."[34]

For the Cambridge Public Library crowdsourcing has provided an important service by improving the searchability of its newspaper collection. The library has been able to improve the database without paying large amounts to contract the work. Crowdsourcing has also changed the way people interact with documents and has encouraged use of the microfilm collection.

Connecting People and History

Inviting the public to assist in this type of project can make good financial sense, but it also serves another purpose. Crowdsourcing provides users with a chance to contribute to common resources while working very closely with the source material. In an interview Nicole Snyder, head of digital library services at the University of Iowa Libraries, stated: "The transcriptionists actually follow the story told in these manuscripts and often become invested in the story or motivated by the thought of furthering research by making these written texts accessible."[35] One transcriber has become so invested in the lives of people mentioned in diaries that he feels they have "become almost an extended part of his family" and mourns their deaths.[36] When turning to the crowd for help you are also providing an opportunity for users to dig into a subject, whether it is a handwritten diary, newspaper articles, or local photographs.

CASE STUDY ■ ■ ↘

COMMUNITY INVOLVEMENT

The Allen County Public library opened in 1895 with a collection of 3,606 books. Originally called the Fort Wayne Public Library, it has grown significantly and currently serves over 355,000 residents. The library has an annual operating budget of approximately $25 million and circulation of over ten million items each year. There are 13 branch libraries and the entire library system employs 237 full-time staff, 154 part-time staff, and a small army of volunteers. Studios for public television broadcasting, an art gallery, and a genealogical center are all part of the main library building, which is a 367,000-square-foot modern structure filled with public art, large windows, and a futuristic blue reading tower in the children's area. This very modern library building embraces the future while preserving important historical collections within.

The Allen County Public Library has worked to engage the community by being the main repository of local historic material, utilizing well-organized volunteers, inviting the public to take part in events to document current events, and increasing access to materials through digitization. As a result users are interacting with library materials as contributors, content creators, and information specialists. These efforts started with the digitization of an important collection of photographs and clippings stored in vertical files, a perfect candidate for an online collection.

The original method of storing these images involved gluing the photos onto cardstock. These pieces of cardstock were acidic and were slowly damaging the images, as was the glue used to attach the photos. These two storage aspects were contributing to the deterioration of the images that were stored in filing cabinets. Those cabinets contained roughly 8,000 images in need of preservation. During this time schools were still sending students for local research projects, making photocopies, and historians and genealogists were pulling files and using the materials as they had in the past. The collection was highly used, and the wear and tear on the materials already compromised by the acidic folders and paper meant a solution would need to be found. A decision was made to digitize the material.

To find volunteers the library reached out to members of the local genealogical society who already were heavy users of the library collection. This allowed the library to pull from a pool of volunteers who were truly interested in the collection and had a strong understanding of how the work they were engaged in would support others who were interested in local and family history. The support of the genealogical society provided workers, some funding, and an appreciative audience for the library's digital collections.

Providing an example of the type of work managed by the library, the presentation and usability of the materials has also encouraged the creation of other projects. When local schools saw the materials the library was making available, it triggered conversations on how the schools could work with the library to digitize school newspapers. One of the oldest schools, South Side High School, had materials dating to the 1920s while some of the newer schools' collections started in the 1970s.

Request for Contemporary Images

For Curt Witcher of the Allen County Public Library, "what is exciting to me is community engagement." For Allen County part of that engagement is a photography contest titled "A Day in Allen County." In 2014 the Allen County community was encouraged to take a photograph on the last day of summer. The library used its network of contacts to reach schools, art teachers, and the local universities (Indiana University and Purdue University satellite campus) to encourage students to participate. Not only does this provide students with a venue for their work, but it shows a young generation that the library, as an institution, values their work and builds on the relationship with these young library users.

One collection which is part of the modern documentation of life in the Fort Wayne area is based on the photographs the library solicited after the devastating storms in 2012. Within the photographs collected are telephone poles broken like twigs and cars flipped and scattered like children's toys illustrating the violence of the storm. The images document the local damage from the point of view of those who lived through the events. Witcher says the library provides individuals with "outlets to experience something, share something." In 2012 a windstorm struck the flooded area and many people lost electricity for weeks. The library asked for people to share images of the damage in their neighborhoods. The result was hundreds of images documenting the destruction.

Another annual event is a poetry contest where, according to Witcher, "there are middle schoolers that just absolutely get geeked about our poetry contest every fall." The Friends of the Library provides trophies for those who participate, the library prints volumes of the poems that are available to participants, and a copy is cataloged. Every author is listed in the contents field of the catalog record. This leads to excitement and pride among the children who are excited to search for their names in the library catalog. Copies of the books from 2008, 2012, and 2013 are available online through the Internet Archive. Each volume contains winners from different grade levels K–12, and participants come from different area schools.

Drinking from the Fire Hose

The Allen County Public Library jumped into the digitization world early, and although it may have been helpful to have had more examples and resources to draw from, the most unexpected issue to arise was not related to technology, workflows, or training, but the flood of interest and materials from the community. Witcher wished that "I would have known that our biggest challenge would be drinking from a fire hose, because we have so much that the community would like us to do." This inundation of material has required the library to prioritize what is scanned. There is plenty of material that can be added solely from the library's historical collection, but other materials are part of collaborative agreements, like the school newspapers, have short deadlines such as the church records which had to be returned, or are of great interest such as the World War I letters. These materials have been determined to be high priority. A collection of firefighting photos was of considerable interest and had a dedicated volunteer who was willing to do the work. Another collection from the General Electric plant has also been added. The plant employed close to 30,000 people during the World War II and Korean War efforts making many electrical devices for the army. The plant also had a building full of records that were to be moved to Tennessee or New York. Of all the challenges a library could possibly face, having a reputation for digitizing and being sought out for more projects is one the library is happy to have. Because of the library's successful outreach efforts it is often the first place people turn to when they find historic documents.

The Allen County Public Library has sought out different segments of the community from local historians to school children. They have created collections based on Lincoln, war letters, and current events. They have used traditional outreach methods such as providing educational events at the library, and the result is a strong reputation and a collection that has led to individuals from across the country contacting the library "without worrying about how do I get the interlibrary loan or how do I get to Fort Wayne." For Witcher "that is the most exciting part in that particular collection, we've really just been on a blazing trail to see how much we can forward face quickly. To me that makes my day, my week, and my month." ■■■

Chapter Synopsis

Outreach is an important tool for gathering materials, metadata, and goodwill from your community. Community involvement is a way to encourage the mission and values of the library and shows that your library believes in protecting local history. Additionally, when the library actively works to involve the community in a project, it reinforces the relationship with the community and provides individuals with a personal connection to the collection.

Benefits of outreach:
- Inviting members to share their personal collections, stories, and knowledge shows the library cares about both the history and the individuals in the community.
- Community efforts can increase the community's valuation of the material and imbue a sense of ownership.
- Your community can assist in providing metadata, saving staff time.

Accurate reflection of the community:
- Check your collections for any gaps regarding time periods or representation of the community.
- Gaps can be filled through outreach efforts.
- People will value an institution that is perceived to value them.

Crowdsourcing:
- Has been found to be highly accurate.
- People are willing to work on crowdsourced projects to help themselves and others.
- Is particularly useful for gathering metadata and correcting OCR transcripts and has been successfully used to improve the searchability of newspapers.

NOTES

1. Tami Oliphant, "I'm a Library Hugger!: Public Libraries as Valued Community Assets," *Public Library Quarterly* 33, no. 4 (2014): 348–61, doi: 10.1080/01616846 .2014.970431.
2. Cathy De Rosa et al., *Perceptions of Libraries: Context and Community* (Dublin, OH: Online Computer Library Center, 2011), 42, www.oclc.org/content/dam/oclc/ reports/2010perceptions/2010perceptions_all_singlepage.pdf.
3. Denise Davis, "Research Statistics on Libraries and Librarianship in 2006," *Bowker Annual Library and Book Trade Almanac,* 2007; *Public Libraries in the United States Survey: Fiscal Year 2012* (Washington, DC: Institute of Museum and Library Services, 2012), www.imls.gov/assets/1/AssetManager/Fast_Facts_PLS_FY2012.pdf.
4. Wendy Liu and David Gal, "Bringing Us Together or Driving Us Apart: The Effect of Soliciting Consumer Input on Consumers' Propensity to Transact with an Organization," *Journal of Consumer Research* 38, no. 2 (2011): 242–59.
5. Alexander Maxwell, "Digital Archives and History Research: Feedback from an End? User," *Library Review* 59, no. 1 (2010): 24-39.

6. LeRoy Charles Merritt, "Readers Open Forum," *Library Journal*, June 15 (1936): 467.

7. Louise S. Robbins, *The Dismissal of Miss Ruth Brown: Civil Rights, Censorship, and the American Library* (Norman: University of Oklahoma Press, 2000); David Battles, *The History of Public Library Access for African Americans in the South, or Leaving Behind the Plow*, (Lanham, MD: Scarecrow, 2009).

8. *Brown v. Louisiana*, 383 U.S. 131 (1966), http://laws.findlaw.com/us/383/131.html.

9. Martha Menchaca, *The Mexican Outsiders: A Community History of Marginalization and Discrimination in California* (Austin: University of Texas Press, 1995).

10. J. G. Parke, "Lieutenant Parke's Route—San Gorgonio Pass," *Reports of Explorations and Surveys, to Ascertain the Most Practicable and Economical Route for a Railroad from the Mississippi River to the Pacific Ocean*, United States War Dept. 5 (1855–60), 36.

11. Bill Bell, *The Black Pioneers of the San Gorgonio Pass, Part 1: A Look at the History of the Black Community in Banning from the 1940s to 1965* (Banning, CA: Banning Library), www.banninglibrarydistrict.org/banning/documents/the%20black%20 pioneers,%20part%201.pdf.

12. Stacia Glenn, "Senate Bill Would Permit Banning School, Library Districts to Separate," *The Sun*, April 20, 2005, http://infoweb.newsbank.com/resources/doc/ nb/news/109998A56DB5C5F2?p=AWNB.

13. Marc Olivier, "George Eastman's Modern Stone-Age Family: Snapshot Photography and the Brownie," *Technology and Culture* 48, no. 1 (2007): 1.

14. "Digital Archiving Tool to Give Indigenous Communities a Voice," *States News Service,* (April 20, 2010).

15. Kathy Kobayashi and Carolyn Kozo Cole, "Ethnic Los Angeles Through Family Albums," *Chronicle of Higher Education* 43, no. 17 (1996): B9.

16. "Project Summary," Shades of LA grant documentation provided by Christina Rice, senior librarian, Los Angeles Public Library Photo Collection.

17. Ibid.

18. Enrique Estelles-Arolas and Fernando Gonzalez-Ladron-de-Guevara, "Towards an Integrated Crowdsourcing Definition," *Journal of Information Science* 38, no. 2 (2012): 189–200.

19. David Gauntlett, *Making Is Connecting: The Social Meaning of Creativity, From DIY and Knitting to YouTube and Web 2.0* (Malden, MA: Polity, 2011).

20. Brian Geiger and Frederick Zarndt, "What Motivates Library Crowdsourcing Volunteers?," American Library Association Conference Presentation (June 30, 2013): 72, www.slideshare.net/cowboyMontana/what-motivates-library -crowdsourcing-volunteers-20130630-ala-lita.

21. Frederick Zarndt, Brian Geiger, Alyssa Pacy, and Stefan Boddie, *Crowdsourcing the World's Cultural Heritage: Part II* (Singapore: IFLA World Library and Information Congress, 2013), 16, www.ifla.org/files/assets/newspapers/Singapore_2013 _papers/day_2_06_2013_ifla_satellite_zarndt_et_al_crowdsourcing_the_worlds _cultural_heritage-_part_ii.pdf.

22. Geiger and Zarndt, "What Motivates Library Crowdsourcing Volunteers?" 85.

23. William Eggers, "Crowd-Sourcing Social Problems," *Reason* 45, no. 8 (January 2014): 44–50.

24. Oded Nov, "What Motivates Wikipedians?" *Communications of the ACM* 50, no. 11 (November 2007): 60-64, doi: 10.1145/1297797.1297798, http://doi.acm.org/ 10.1145/1297797.1297798.

25. Stacey Kuznetsov, "Motivations of Contributors to Wikipedia," *ACM SIGCAS Computers and Society* 36, no. 2 (June 2006).

26. Michekke Springer et al., "*For the Common Good: The Library of Congress Flickr Pilot Project*" (Washington, DC: Library of Congress, October 30, 2008), 15, www.loc .gov/rr/print/flickr_report_final.pdf.

27. Geiger and Zarndt. "What Motivates Library Crowdsourcing Volunteers?" 46–49.

28. Ibid., 55.

29. J. Nahapiet and S. Ghoshal, "Social Capital, Intellectual Capital, and the Organizational Advantage," *Academy of Management Review* 23, no. 2 (1998): 242–66.

30. Ben Verhbow, "NYPD Labs: Hacking the Library," *Journal of Library Administration* 53, no. 1 (January 2015): 79–96, doi: 10.1080/01930826.2013.756701.

31. Ibid.

32. "Help," Cambridge Public Library website, http://cambridge.dlconsulting.com/ cgi-bin/cambridge?a=p&p=help&e=-------en-20--1--txt-txIN------#all.

33. Alyssa Pacy, *Newspapers in the Digital Age: A Case Study in How Public Library Patrons Read the News* (Lyon, France: IFLA World Library and Information Conference, 2014), 11, www.ifla.org/files/assets/newspapers/Geneva_2014/s6-pacy-en.pdf.

34. Ibid., 14-15.

35. Bill LeFurgy, "Crowdsourcing the Civil War: Insights Interview with Nicole Saylor," *The Signal* blog (December 6, 2011), http://blogs.loc.gov/digitalpreservation/ 2011/12/crowdsourcing-the-civil-war-insights-interview-with-nicole-saylor/.

36. Ibid.

CHAPTER 5

FUNDING OPPORTUNITIES

Anytime somebody wants to give me money, I say yes.

—Wanda Marget, director of the Fairmont Public Library, Nebraska

You would love to digitize materials in your collection but where do you find the money? Digitization can be expensive and your library may not have funding for these activities as part of your annual budget. This has not stopped many libraries from completing successful projects. Volunteers can perform amazing amounts of work and partnering with institutions can be a great way to reduce costs, but you still need a budget. Grants from state and federal agencies, foundations, individuals, and your community can provide this funding.

FEDERAL GRANTS

Federal and state grants are available to libraries and cultural institutions for digitization programs. The Institute of Museum and Library Services (IMLS) provides a number of grants like the National Leadership Grants for Libraries which can provide funding for research, planning, or national forums. Depending on the type of grant, these competitive awards can be as high as $2 million for projects and research. In 2014 there were 98 applicants for Leadership grants, with 19 grants awarded amounting to $6,969,176 in project grants going to different institutions and over $6 million in matching funding.[1] Over $2 million was awarded to 12 planning proposals. These grants are frequently sought by university libraries which make up the majority of projects funded, but institutions, societies, museums, and other educational organization also apply for these grants. (See figure 5.1.)

FIGURE 5.1

National Leadership Grants for Libraries Awarded by Institution Type

Year[i]	Total Number of Grants	Universities/Colleges	Public Libraries	Other
2010	34	20	3	11
2011	40	29	2	9
2012	52	22	13	17
2013	40	20	9	11
2014	36	15	6	15

i. Awarded Grants search. National Leadership Grants for Libraries. IMLS. www.imls.gov/recipients/grantsearch.aspx.

Institute of Museum and Library Services

These grant amounts can be very large. The public library projects which are funded tend to be collaborations with other institutions and are requested by library consortia, systems, or institutions working with other groups. One reason for this may be the expectation of matching funds or in-kind contributions from the requesting organization. Requests for funding over $250,000 "must provide cost sharing of at least one-half of the total project cost, excluding funds for student support" and "may be supported by your cash outlays; contribution of property and services; and in-kind contributions, such as staff or volunteer time that support project activities."[2] Another reason why these grants tend to go to collaborative projects is because some grants like those for leadership are intended to support a national digital platform or bridge gaps between collections and infrastructure. Currently the National Leadership Grants for Libraries is not supporting the digitization of content but these grants can be used, however, for plans on the preservation of digital files and for technology tools. Individual libraries do obtain these grants but it is not common.

In 2013 the Buffalo and Erie County Public Library system in New York state received over $300,000 for a two-year project to "demonstrate the concept of a 'digitized commons' that emphasizes selection and digitization of collections that are tied directly to virtual and physical activities and events that encourage local civic engagement."[3] This grant was the result of years of effort starting with a project to create an inventory of Great Depression and New Deal-era resources in the community. This work led to a $25,000 National Endowment for the Humanities start-up grant in 2009 to show "how digital humanities can help a public library mobilize collections to address the civic purposes central to its mission."[4] Success with previous grants encouraged the library to try for a larger IMLS grant, a process which Anne Conable, the community engagement manager, initially found "absolutely terrifying."

The process required significant preparation just for writing the grant. Their first attempt at requesting IMLS funds was denied, but the feedback from the reviewer showed them where to strengthen the document. After completely rewriting the proposal it was accepted. Working with a number of partners who contributed in-kind matches Conable managed the grant, working regularly with IMLS staff as the project developed and changed. She found the staff there to be very supportive when new partners were added to the project. As the program progressed the subject expanded from the New Deal to include the Hispanic Heritage Council of Western New York, which had started collecting stories from the Hispanic community.

The most challenging part of this process for Conable was the writing of the grant. This required a comprehensive understanding of the project, the partners, outcomes, and the collection of information such as curriculum vitae for individuals involved. The month before the proposal was due Conable worked on little else. After receiving the funding she spent between 10 and 15 percent of her time documenting, editing the budget, and reporting on progress. The partners, who are under contract with the library, submit periodic invoices and their own documentation which must be managed. Although she has not found this process onerous, it has required regular attention.

The benefits of this grant, beyond the funding, include the support offered by the IMLS staff and the increased visibility and prestige that comes from obtaining this type of grant. With considerable competition involved, being able to show your library obtained one of these large grants is enough to garner attention and a reputation as the type of library which can meet the high standards of the IMLS. Winning this grant has also made the library less timid about trying for larger grants and has encouraged the library to think more creatively about funding opportunities.

For other libraries considering trying for these grants Conable recommends that they plan well in advance of the deadline. You will need to prove your case in the documentation you provide and need to have a clear vision of what will be done, the purpose of the project, who your partners will be, and you need to have a detailed budget. Make sure you will be able to invest the time required to write and manage the grant. If you have received other grants related to the project, these can help show the IMLS reviewers that other organizations have also supported your efforts.

Native American Library Services: Enhancement Grants

If you work in a tribal library there are IMLS grants which can be used for digital projects. The Native American Library Services: Enhancement Grants are open to "Indian tribes, Alaska native villages, regional corporations, and village corporations [which] are eligible to apply for funding under the Native American Library Services grant program."[5] The Jamestown S'Klallam Tribal Library in Sequim, Washington, has worked to create online content since 1998 when director Leanne Jenkins first realized the potential of using a website to bring collections to tribal members near and far. Using portions of their IMLS Services Grant for scanning services, they were able to start building their digital collection. Wishing to enhance the collection, the library carefully crafted a proposal for an IMLS Enhancement grant in 2007. According to Jenkins, the grant writing required the library to balance "the desire to do everything at once with the realities of what was feasible to do within the time frame and budget."[6] The resulting collection, which was completed in 2009, was called House of Seven Generations and has almost 6,000 items in 27 different collections.

The library received another enhancement grant in 2011 for $150,000 to "generate cultural and educational tools" based on the in-house collections and incorporating the House of Seven Generations.[7] With IMLS support the library has continued to add to the collection in a way director Jenkins compares to a wood carver "chipping away at . . . and drawing out the shapes and forms that will tell our stories to the world."[8]

LSTA Funds

The most common digitization grants accessed by libraries are Library Services and Technology Act (LSTA) grants. These funds are distributed through the Institute of Museum and Library Services as part of the Grants to State Library Administrative Agencies (SLAA). This program goes back to 1956 with the passage of the Library Services Act. The original act was intended to "promote the further extension by the several States of public library services to rural areas without such services or with inadequate services."[9] In 1962 the type of library which could receive these funds was expanded beyond rural libraries and was tied to Title II (the section of the Code of Federal Regulations dealing with Grants and Agreements), allowing funding for construction and remodeling. By 1996 the program shifted with emphasis placed on technology, which is the focus of the current LSTA program.

Each SLAA receives a base amount of $680,000 plus an additional amount based upon the population of the state.[10] The funds can be used for statewide initiatives or are awarded in a competitive process. These grants are sometimes rebranded, such as TexTreasures, which are LSTA grants administered by the Texas State Library and Archives Commission as part of the TexShare program. TexShare is "a consortium of Texas libraries joining together to share print and electronic materials, purchase online resources, and combine staff expertise."[11]

Among the priorities of the LSTA program are to improve services, facilitate access, encourage resource sharing, promote literacy, and ensure preservation. Many of these aspects are included in digitization programs which preserve, improve access, and include elements of resource sharing. Training and professional development for library staff is also supported.

The Power of One (Grant Writer)

Sue Adams of the Oregon City Library wanted to make her library's newspapers more accessible since 1995. At that time she noticed that the library regularly received requests from people looking for information in the local newspaper. These requests for obituaries, local events, and history were often lacking a specific date and with indexes for only a few years at their disposal, finding what the users wanted would be very difficult. At first Adams considered adding to the index, thinking "maybe if I spent an hour every day looking through the microfilm I could do it." As new technologies emerged like CD-ROMs she hoped that a company might provide an index, but it wasn't until the Oregon Digital Newspaper Program began that there seemed to be a real chance to provide the type of access she knew her patrons wanted. The Digital Newspaper Program was started by the University of Oregon and funded by grants from the National Endowment for the Humanities and Library of Congress, Oregon State Historic Preservation Office and Oregon Heritage Commission, and a Library Services and Technology block grant from the IMLS. The goal of the program was to provide access to a database of keyword-searchable newspapers from 1860 to 1922.

Adams was eager to have Oregon City newspapers included. Never underestimate a single person with a goal and the drive to see a project through. With the support of her director, Adams began working on the grant while stationed at the reference desk because "basically this . . . was the only way we could do it." In early November 2012 the library learned that the project would be funded in the following year although there was a delay due to the federal government closure. The shutdown caused "some biting of the fingernails" but the library soon received permission to spend. The university handled all the scanning and technical issues but there were reports to write, handouts to develop, and programs to plan around the new collection. Being awarded the grant is just one part of the grant process. The management, promotion, and reports also require considerable time. Sue Adams estimates that she and her director spent between 45 to 50 hours writing the grant and another 50 hours to gather materials, write three quarterly reports, and a final report.

Her time on the reference desk gave Adams insight into the usage of the collection and provided contacts with others inside and outside of the community who supported the goal to digitize the newspapers. One patron from Texas who was using the collection even contributed a letter of support for the grant. More letters of support came as the project progressed and the community was introduced to the new format for an old and popular resource. The grant provided the funding needed to outsource the digitization and metadata creation and allowed a library with an already busy staff to make a significant contribution to the Oregon Digital Newspaper program.

National Endowment for the Humanities

The National Endowment for the Humanities (NEH) has several grants including the National Digital Newspaper Program, which funds large institutions and consortia in each state. These grants fund the digitization of newspapers for inclusion in Chronicling America, which is hosted by the Library of Congress. These grants may be redistributed by the state agencies. There is another grant which is open to public libraries of all sizes.

The Humanities Collections and Reference Resources grant has, from 2000 to 2012, allowed institutions to reformat 80,000 hours of audio and video collections, process or digitize thousands of feet of archival material, and digitize "more than 2.3 million books, manuscripts, photos, maps, drawings, [and] other nonprint materials."[12] The Division of Preservation and Access has made the digital conversion of audio files a priority because the deterioration of magnetic tape and other formats combined with the obsolescence of technology used to access the material "seriously jeopardize their use."[13] These grants are available to public libraries and are competitive. An average of 237 applications are received each year but only 16 percent of them are awarded.[14]

National Historical Publications and Records Commission

The grant program from the National Historical Publications and Records Commission has a variety of grants for projects seeking to increase public interaction, facilitate public discovery, and disseminate digital versions of historical records. The Digital Dissemination of Archival Collections grant seeks to "to make historical records of national significance to the United States broadly available by disseminating digital surrogates on the Internet."[15] Although this agency focuses on archives, public libraries have received these grants. The Atlanta-Fulton Public Library System in Atlanta, Georgia, received $58,710 in 2010 to digitize manuscripts "documenting the role of African Americans in educational institutions."[16] Eleven collections were digitized and are available on the website for the Auburn Avenue Research Library on African American Culture and History. If your library has an archive or historic collection it may be worth investigating these grants.

STATE GRANTS

There are other, non-LSTA, state-level grants which may be available to you. The Illinois State Library has a Digital Imaging Grant Program. The funding for this program is a combination of LSTA and state funds from the Office of the Secretary of State/Illinois State Librarian. Grants range from between $5,000 and $100,000 and digital materials are ingested into the Illinois Digital Archive. In 2015 over $400,000 was awarded to 13 organizations including eight public libraries. Awards ranged from $5,521 to the Huntley Area Public Library District in Huntley for the "preservation and digitization of the dairy and agricultural history of Huntley" to $86,919 for the Oak Park Public Library's project Hacking Hemingway: Cracking the Code to the Vault.[17]

In New Hampshire the Moose License Plate Conservation Grants provide grants of up to $10,000 to "public institutions with publicly owned documents that are significant to the history of New Hampshire."[18] As the title suggests, these grants are funded by the sale of Moose License Plates. In the 2013/2014 award cycle the Allenstown Public Library received $8,745 for "conservation, microfilm & digitization of 19th century Allenstown poll tax records dated 1860–1889."[19] These items are available in the Allenstown Digital History website.

Finding Grants

The main resource for locating federal grants is grants.gov, but information is also available on the NEH and IMLS websites. Check with your state library for LSTA and other grant opportunities. If you are unsure of the LSTA administering agency in your state, check the IMLS State Programs, State Profiles database.

FOUNDATIONS

Private foundations are another possible source of funding. These range from small, local nonprofit organizations to large, international foundations like the Bill & Melinda Gates Foundation. Unlike IMLS grants, the requirements for a foundation grant can vary widely. How can you find this type of financial support? Local organizations are an important place to start since they may already be interested in increasing access to your collection. When looking for support outside of your community, foundations will often look to see if your library has received local support. Even small grants provide proof that the people who know your organization trust you enough to help fund your goals. Even if the amount you receive is small, this local support can improve your chances of convincing outside groups to support you.

Local foundations may support your library with funding or equipment. Mary Cronin, former director of the Madison Public Library in New Hampshire, found when seeking funding for equipment that "the local foundations are usually pretty supportive of this sort of project. . . . I had no problem getting funding for software and hard drives, and an audio recorder." With local foundations you have several advantages which increase your chances of receiving support: foundations tend to give locally and will already have an idea of your goals and mission.

When looking outside of your community, keep in mind that many foundations limit their funding to specific geographical locations. This will narrow down the number of places where you should apply but can also increase your chances of succeeding because these foundations have less competition than organizations which give nationally or internationally. Foundations will also have specific missions and areas of interest they support.

The Georgetown Public Library and eight other libraries were able to obtain a grant for $350,000 from the Gaylord and Dorothy Donnelley Foundation in 2006. This foundation is interested in supporting collections "that illuminate the unique culture, history and heritage" and only accepts applications from the Chicago region or the Lowcountry of South Carolina.[20] Both the location

(Georgetown is in South Carolina) and the goal of the library worked well with the mission of this foundation. Other grants came from the Belle W. Baruch Foundation of Georgetown, which gives to educational projects and does not accept unsolicited requests, and the Kaminski House Museum.[21] The Baruch Foundation and the Kaminski House are nonprofits located in Georgetown and both were already familiar with the library.

A Little Help from a Friend

In Texas if you do not seek partnerships for digitizing newspapers the opportunities may find you instead. Librarians at the University of North Texas (UNT) in Denton have been working to build a comprehensive database of newspapers by digitizing collections around the state. Ana Krahmer, supervisor for the digital newspaper unit, wrote "for the Portal, we decided to spread the message that we were interested in digitizing all Texas newspaper content, whether it came from a town of 600 people, or whether it represented Fort Worth, Texas, during its cattle boom."[22] The need to preserve state history through digitizing state newspapers led the libraries to take on the role of a preservation and digitization hub. There are libraries throughout Texas with primary source materials which Krahmer hopes to add to the Portal to Texas History, and if libraries do not know of programs' services she may seek them out.

The University of North Texas has worked closely with libraries to secure funding. According to Krahmer, in some cases, when a library is seeking a grant the "granting foundations will have them contact us." In one partnership the library has been working with the Tocker Foundation, which supports Texas libraries in communities with populations under 12,000.[23] This partnership started when the foundation was unhappy with the amount of materials being digitized through its grants. Krahmer related that in 2007 UNT libraries approached the Tocker Foundation with a proposal to scan materials for libraries that received grants and add those collections to the already established Portal to Texas History. This partnership has been so successful that the foundation works exclusively with the university to support the needs of these libraries.

UNT Libraries work closely with public libraries to help them get Tocker grants and the foundation will often refer libraries to UNT where, Krahmer states, the public libraries can expect assistance "with preparing their applications, . . . creating a budget for the project, developing a map of where their microfilm is held or where their physical newspapers are held." In some cases a librarian will travel to the institution to pick up material for scanning or to work directly with the staff.

An additional benefit is that the libraries who join the Portal to Texas History have access to detailed usage statistics generated by an in-house program at the University of North Texas Libraries. The program counts the number of items a user has viewed or interacted with for at least thirty minutes, providing helpful information regarding use. With a little or a lot of help libraries in Texas can work with UNT to get their newspapers online.

This partnership has resulted in over 315,000 pages of newspapers available on the Portal with 100,000 being digitized in 2013. The collections "represent(s) eighteen communities from across Texas whose public library directors have applied to receive digitization grant funding to make their newspapers available on the Portal to Texas History."[24] Some other National Digital Newspaper Program libraries may offer assistance to smaller libraries; the Pennsylvania State University Libraries helps smaller institutions by reviewing grant applications and providing technical support. If you are considering digitizing your newspaper collections, contact your state NDNP library regarding possible grant assistance.

Finding Foundations

Where should you start looking for foundation grants? Start with organizations which already have a relationship with or knowledge of your efforts; this includes your Friends of the Library foundations. If your goals and the mission of the organization are similar there is a good chance they will consider your proposal. There are tools which can help you locate foundations; one is the Foundation Center Directory, a database of foundations around the country. The database allows users to use very specific search criteria to find nonprofits which provide funding to public libraries.

Other organizations and individuals have compiled lists of available grants. Stephanie Gerding and Pam MacKellar, authors of *Winning Grants: A How-to-Do-It Manual for Librarians with Mulitimedia Tutorials and Grant Development Tools* (2010) maintain a blog with notices for current grant opportunities.

INDIVIDUALS AND GIFTS

If you can bring an interested donor and a collection together that may be all that is needed to fund your project. In Bangor, Maine, it was the collection which found the donor. Barbara McDade, director of the Bangor Public Library and Joyce Rumery, dean of libraries at the University of Maine, were meeting with Senator Susan Collins at the Public Library. On display for the senator were some samples from a collection of war posters collected by former librarian L. Felix Ranlett during his twenty-six years at the Bangor Public Library. Ranlett was a veteran who had fought and was wounded in the trenches of France during World War I. In 1936 he moved from Boston to Bangor and began working at the public library. During World War II he began to collect the posters distributed by government agencies and businesses. The extensive collection was kept on shelves in an area in the basement known as "the cage" where the posters were rarely seen and were feeling the effects of time.

Later, over coffee, Dean Rumery mentioned the collection to Eugene Daigle, the manager of network and technology services for the Fogler Library at the University of Maine. Daigle was interested in the posters. He knew of some similar online collections (Northwestern University in Illinois has a collection of 338 posters) and was excited to learn that his local public library also had war-related posters. Eugene met with McDade and learned that the materials in "the cage" were far more extensive than he had expected, with over 800 posters from both world wars, making it possibly one of the largest collections of its kind in America. In comparison, the Library of Congress has 119 posters from World War II in the Prints & Photographs Online Catalog. If the Bangor collection was digitized it would be a great resource.

The condition of the collection had been a concern since the 1990s. Some preservation measures had been taken but were limited by staff and budget issues. The posters had been printed at a time when paper drives were required to meet the demand for the military effort. The recycled paper used for many of the posters is acidic, resulting in the paper becoming increasingly brittle over time. Handling can result in breakage. Originally the library focused on preserving the paper and digitization was not considered. The prospect of being able to provide access to digital copies to limit handling and providing assistance to preserve the originals was very tempting.

The collection had considerable meaning for Daigle. He and his wife, Barbara, are veterans. His father had served in the Korean War and his father-in-law was a veteran of World War II. The posters serve as a connection to the past, a reminder of the efforts at home to support the war, and are a visual backdrop of the era. These are images World War II veterans and their families would have been familiar with. Daigle stated that the reason he and his wife wanted to make these posters available was "to allow people born after World War II to look at these artworks and try to get a sense of the conflict and how each and every citizen was asked to contribute to the war effort—to help their sons, daughters, fathers, mothers, brothers, sisters, and cousins defeat the Axis powers. . . . Every neighborhood was involved in the war effort, and these posters are part of the voice of the people who were part of the final victory in August of 1945."[25] These posters of Red Cross nurses with open arms and angelic expressions, Norman Rockwell's Lincolnesque figure standing for the freedom of speech and war bonds, children halted in their play while the shadow of a swastika spreads on the grass around them, and men and women in uniform with determined expressions were created to encourage everything from enlistment to recycling cooking fat. Depictions of Nazi book burning and Pearl Harbor were meant to remind people why they were fighting. The posters document the war effort, the home front, and depict patriotism and vigilance. These images also provide examples of propaganda, depictions of women during war, advertising methods, and examples of artistic styles. As a whole the collections provides insight as to what life was like in the United States during both wars.

Daigle and his wife Barbara offered to pay for digitization, which required high-quality photography of the posters. That job fell to Eugene's brother, James, who is a professional photographer. Because this was the first digitization project for the library, there were technical issues which had to be worked out. Library staff worked with James to create a space where the images could be captured. To photograph the posters without causing any damage he created a special vacuum table to gently hold the paper in place.

Eugene Daigle also donated his time to process the digital images and create multiple files of different sizes. One aspect of their process which was different from other digitized poster collections at that time was the creation of larger image files. Most digital collections of war posters only contain small thumbnail images that don't allow the user to see the detail or have a sense of the visual impact of the piece. After work Eugene would process the images, creating several file sizes: thumbnails for browsing, a medium size which shows more detail, and larger files for printing reproductions.

Daigle works at the University of Maine library, which was willing to host the digital collection and make it freely accessible. In addition to online access, the public can purchase copies of the posters for $19.95. Posters are printed by the university with the funds going towards the preservation of the original posters, which will be stored in acid-free folders in map cases at the Bangor Public Library.

This improved access has resulted in increased awareness of the library's collection. As the project progressed Daigle's father shared the images with other veterans at the Togus Veterans' Administration hospital and the American Legion. After the collection was made publicly available, the National Park Service requested a digital set of posters for a special ranger program at the World War II Memorial in Washington, DC. Visitors to the Cole Museum in Bangor can see a slide show of all the posters. Interest in the collection has spread beyond the state, with some academic libraries such as Utah State University and Shawnee State University in Ohio including links to the collection among their own resources.

CASE STUDY

FUND-RAISING FOR A NEWSPAPER COLLECTION

In 2008 *Library Journal* named the Chelsea Public Library in Michigan as the Best Small Library in America. The staff was described as "aggressively responsive" which, with other qualities, led to "victories in fundraising and elections have garnered the money to modernize and double the size of the historic building, add to the staff, and serve the whole community."[26] Chelsea became a city in 2006 and the U.S. Census estimates the 2014 population to be 5,106. The library, however, serves twice this number, with the library district encompassing the surrounding townships of Dexter, Lima, Lyndon, and Sylvan and about 14,000 people.

The library is in a historic hotel left to the city (then town) by Catherine McKune in 1958 specifically for use as a library.[27] Eventually the library outgrew the location and needed an expansion, which was added in 2006. The library now houses 66,142 items and in 2008 its circulation was 313,295.[28] The majority of the collections are in the newer, ADA-compliant, 18,000-square-foot addition. The older section of the library was renovated through a capital campaign that raised $1.2 million.

If the library staff is "aggressively responsive" the community it serves is equally supportive. When the staff wanted to digitize the library's newspapers they knew it could be expensive. Emily Meloche, adult services librarian, recalled that "it was one of those projects that we dreamed about doing and when we found out how much it was going to cost we knew we had to get creative with how we could fund it." The library had received grants in the past for oral histories, but rather than pursue that path they looked for support from a community where many families have lived in the area for 100 years and are deeply invested in the city. The library staff were sure that there would be support because of the strong community interest in local history. The bound volumes in the basement dated back to the late nineteenth century and the rolls of microfilm brought the collection up to the current date. Of those early newspapers Meloche noted that the old newspapers were a wonderful source of information but these large, bound newspapers were brittle and the microfilm, "while it is a wonderful thing to have . . . is still a real pain in the neck to use." The movement of the images cause some people to become nauseous after using the microfilm for an extended period of time. Although microfilm is a good medium for preservation, the format is not user-friendly when compared to electronic formats. If you are lucky someone may have created an index for a number of years, but the time needed to scroll or maneuver to the correct page and locate the information needed is glacially slow when compared to an electronic, keyword-searchable document. This is what the library wanted to be able to provide to the community. When the library was able to get copyright permission from the owners of the *Chelsea Standard* up to the 1990s (the newspaper was sold to Heritage in the early 1990s) the library was excited to have the opportunity to digitize the microfilm. When Heritage was contacted regarding copyright, the library was pleasantly surprised to receive permission to digitize up to 2012. The presumed rationale for this was that Heritage sells copies of the photos seen in the newspaper. Digitized copies of the microfilm are not of a quality that would hinder sales of those images.

Changing the manner of access from microfilm with in-library use and specialized viewing equipment to free online access would make the collection far more accessible for the whole library district, especially those in the surrounding townships. Historically the microfilm was used by genealogists and a small number of local historians. These users are willing to spend an extended amount of time to locate marriage announcements and other specific scraps of information. Meloche believed that by putting the paper online and making it searchable for casual users more students and people around the world be able to enjoy the newspaper. For Meloche making the paper available online meant people would have the opportunity to "see world history unfolding through the lens of our local community."[29] The Great Depression, world wars, and events large and small can all be read from the perspective of a Michigan town.

Excited about increasing the accessibility of an already popular resource, the library sought bids for the work "and found a pretty competitive bid of 12 cents a page, but 12 cents a page for 134 years' worth of newspapers was far more than our local history budget, far more than we would ask our friends for." Based on the level of interest and the general support of the community, Meloche and others decided to look to the community for the needed funding. The challenge was to find the best way to raise the funds for digitization. In looking at the amount of scanning required, dividing the collection by year was a simple way to break up the extensive newspaper into years for "134 sponsorship opportunities." It was determined that a sponsorship of $100 per year of the paper would provide enough to have a year's worth of the paper digitized while keeping the price at a realistic amount for many people to donate. These individual years would also resonate with individuals as birth years or have other personal significance. Instead of looking for a few large donors the library sought to find many people who wanted to be part of the project.

On August 3, 2013, the library held the first-ever fund-raising event called Barn-Bash: Making Hay for the Library. The event was held at Sensoli Liberty Farm, a barbeque dinner was catered, and a local band provided music. The event was successful, which did not surprise Meloche, who grew up in Chelsea and knew how the community would come together for this type of enterprise. What she did find surprising was how swiftly the community embraced this project: "I was shocked at how quickly people came and signed up for years." By November 2013 nearly 60 percent of the funds needed had been raised.[30] The library suggested sponsors could "pick the birth year of someone special, an anniversary, or just a year in history that piques your interest, and make it available to the world."[31]

The library is truly grateful to the many people in the community who have sponsored this project. The methods they used to thank these individuals also encourages additional contributions. One simple tool was a sign listing the years with names of donors next to the ones already claimed. This was situated in such a manner that whoever entered the library would have to see the sign. One day a couple entered the library and upon seeing this inquired as to the sign's meaning. Upon learning more about the goal of the digitization project they adopted two years. A few weeks later they claimed more and eventually sponsored a total of nine years. There were several individuals who sponsored multiple years and then later added to their initial donation. As the project progressed more sponsors claimed years, sometimes with the intention of honoring a family member or friends.

By November 2013 all the newspaper had been scanned, but rather than wait for the fund-raising to be completed the library held a launch party on November 10 "to celebrate it [the collection] with our donors and the community and give them an opportunity to check it." This gave the sponsors an opportunity to see the results of their contribution and how the collection would be accessed. The event also served to rejuvenate interest in the project. During this event "we had a couple of our long-term donors come and pick out yet another year." Some donors sponsored six or seven and in one case twelve years' worth of newspapers.

The next day there were only fifteen unclaimed newspaper years, but the expectation was that these would soon find sponsors. Meloche stated, "I'd be shocked if we have any years left by the end of this year." The *Chelsea Standard* published a story on the launch which helped to generate even more interest and the remaining years were soon claimed. Meloche credits the success of the fund-raising to making people "feel important for the donation they made."[32]

In addition to the launch Meloche and other library staff gave presentations on the database to small groups and anyone they ran into around the city. In January 2014 Sara Wedell, who at the time was the library's adult services department head, spoke about the project at the Friends' annual meeting.[33] To show its appreciation the library worked to recognize the donors. The database website includes a list of years and the donors who paid for the digitization. This list has a link in the drop-down menu for the Historic Newspapers and on each search page. The library is also exploring adding a watermark to the first page of each issue of the newspaper which will acknowledge the donor so that users will see the donor name even if users do not access the donor list. The library is serious about making "sure the donors get the credit they deserve because we wouldn't be here without them." This strategy of promoting the projects and offering their sincere thanks to those who contributed worked well. By January 2014 the library had 70 percent of the donations needed.[34] In March 2015 the library director announced that the project was completed.[35]

The library is not currently looking for digitization grants but instead will "wait till we have that idea that we think is well worth asking people for money, and then return to the community." The Chelsea District Library knows it can turn to the community for projects that preserve and highlight local history. ■■■

Chapter Synopsis

Federal and state grants can be a great source of funds. Consider the following:

- **IMLS:** Working with another institution will improve your chances of getting these grants.
- **LSTA:** These grants are administered by state agencies or library consortia. Your library has a good chance of obtaining these grants.
- **NEH:** This agency funds newspaper digitization through the National Digital Newspaper Program. Find the agency in your state which administers this grant. The Humanities Collections and Reference Resources grants are also available but are highly competitive.
- **NHPRC:** The National Historical Publications and Records Commission gives grants for the digitization of archival and historic materials.

- Check with your state library to learn about any state-level grant opportunities.
- There will be paperwork. When considering these grants take into consideration the time needed to write the initial proposal and regular reports.

Foundations and nonprofits are another option for many libraries. To increase your chances of getting these grants:

- Start with local organizations.
- Look for foundations with similar goals and missions.
- Don't forget your Friends!
- Foundations can be found with tools such as the Foundation Center. Check with your state library association for individuals who may maintain a list of foundations which give to libraries.
- An interested individual who sees the value of your collection can be of great help. When possible find individuals in the community who are passionate about your collection.

Fund-raising can be a successful strategy for funding your project. When asking your community to fund a project:

- Do your research, get quotes, and develop a plan before asking for support.
- If possible, break down the amount needed into smaller sponsorships to encourage giving.
- Have a deadline for completion.
- Use your library newsletter, website, signs, and everything in your public relations tool box to promote the campaign.
- Thank your donors and give them credit for their support. Then thank them again!

NOTES

1. "Fast Fact Sheet: National Leadership Grants for Libraries (2014)," Institute of Museum and Library Services website, www.imls.gov/recipients/fast_facts_nlg _for_libraries.aspx.
2. "Instructions for Completing Budget Documents," Institute of Museum and Library Services website, www.imls.gov/applicants/instructions_for_completing _budget_documents.aspx#costshare;
   "National Leadership Grants for Libraries—FY15 Notice of Funding Opportunity," Institute of Museum and Library Services website, www.imls.gov/applicants/nlg .libraries_nofo_2015.aspx.

3. "National Leadership Grants: September 2012 Grant Announcements," Institute of Museum and Library Services website, www.imls.gov/news/national_leadership _grant_announcement_2012.aspx.

4. "Re-Collecting the Depression and New Deal as a Civic Resource in Hard Times," National Endowment for the Humanities, 2010, https://securegrants.neh.gov/ PublicQuery/main.aspx?f=1&gn=HD-50901-09.

5. "Native American Library Services: Enhancement Grants," Institute of Museum and Library Services website, www.imls.gov/applicants/detail.aspx?GrantId=16.

6. Leanne Jenkins, "Chipping Away at It," *UpNext* (September 20, 2013), http://blog .imls.gov/?p=4192.

7. "Awarded Grants Results," Institute of Museum and Library Services website, www.imls.gov/recipients/grantsearch.aspx.

8. Jenkins, "Chipping Away at It."

9. Library Services Act, Pub. L. No. 597, Chapter 407 (June 19, 1956), www.gpo.gov/ fdsys/pkg/STATUTE-70/pdf/STATUTE-70-Pg293.pdf.

10. "Grants to State Library Administrative Agencies," Institute of Museum and Library Services website, www.imls.gov/programs/.

11. "TexShare Fact Sheet," Texas State Library and Archives Commission website, https://www.tsl.texas.gov/texshare/fact_sheet_faqs.html.

12. Nadina Gardner, Ralph Canevali, Joel Wurl, and Cathleen Tefft, "Humanities Collections and Reference Resources: An Evaluation 2000–2010" (Washington, DC: National Endowment for the Humanities, 2013), 3, www.neh.gov/files/divisions/ preservation/hcrr_evaluation_report_2013_0.pdf.

13. Ibid., 8.

14. Ibid.

15. "Digital Dissemination of Archival Collections," National Historical Publications and Records Commission website, www.archives.gov/nhprc/announcement/ digital.html.

16. "Georgia Grants," National Historical Publications & Records Commission website, www.archives.gov/nhprc/projects/states-territories/ga.html.

17. "Jesse White Awards over $400,000 in Illinois History–Digital Imaging Grants," Office of the Secretary of State website (January 7, 2015), www.cyberdriveillinois .com/news/2015/january/150107d1.pdf.

18. "Moose License Plate Conservation Grants 2015/2016," New Hampshire State Library website, www.nh.gov/nhsl/services/librarians/moose/index.html.

19. "FY 2013/2014 Moose Conservation License Plate Grant Awards," New Hampshire State Library website, www.nh.gov/nhsl/services/librarians/moose/documents/ 2013Awardslist.pdf.

20. "Regional Collections," Gaylord and Dorothy Donnelley Foundation website (2015), http://gddf.org/regional-collections.

21. Julie Warren, "Georgetown Library Seeks Public's Help to Preserve the Past in the Digital Age," *MyrtleBeach Online* (August 14, 2013), www.myrtlebeachonline.com/2013/08/14/3645787/letter-georgetown-library-seeks.html; "Belle W. Baruch Foundation," Foundation Directory Online.

22. Ana & Phillips Krahmer and Mark Edward, *Laying the Groundwork for Newspaper Preservation through Collaboration and Communication: The Texas Digital Newspaper Program* (Denton: University of North Texas Libraries Digital Library, 2013), http://digital.library.unt.edu/ark:/67531/metadc172339.

23. "General Grant Information," Tocker Foundation website, www.tocker.org/general-instructions.

24. Krahmer and Phillips, *Laying the Groundwork for Newspaper Preservation through Collaboration and Communication*, 6.

25. Dale McGarrigle, "Library's Wartime Poster Collection Now Digitized, Available to Public," *The Weekly* (December 15, 2011), http://bangordailynews.com/2011/12/15/the-weekly/librarys-wartime-poster-collection-now-digitized-available-to-public.

26. John N Berry III, "Best Small Library in America 2008: Chelsea District Library—A Michigan Model," *Library Journal* (2008), http://lj.libraryjournal.com/awards/best-small-library-in-america-2008-chelsea-district-library-a-michigan-model/.

27. "History of the Chelsea District Library," Chelsea District Library website, www.chelsea.lib.mi.us/history.

28. "Library Information," Chelsea District Library website, www.chelsea.lib.mi.us/library.

29. *Chelsea District Library Director's Report* (Chelsea, MI: Chelsea Public Library District, October 2013), http://chelseadistrictlibrary.org/sites/default/files/boarddocuments/2013/2013_Director_Reports/director1310.pdf.

30. *Chelsea District Library Director's Report* (Chelsea, MI: Chelsea Public Library District, November 2013), http://chelseadistrictlibrary.org/sites/default/files/boarddocuments/2013/2013_Director_Reports/director1311.pdf.

31. Ibid.

32. Jennifer Eberbach, "Chelsea District Library Completes Digital Newspaper Archives Project," *Chelsea Standard* (November 22, 2014), http://heritage.com/articles/2014/11/22/chelsea_standard/news/doc546a5506432de212616367.txt?viewmode=fullstory.

33. *Chelsea District Library Director's Report* (Chelsea, MI: Chelsea Public Library District, January 2014), http://chelseadistrictlibrary.org/sites/default/files/boarddocuments/2014/2014_Director_Reports/director201401.pdf.

34. Chelsea District Library Board of Trustees, *Minutes of Regular Meeting*, January 21, 2014, http://chelseadistrictlibrary.org/sites/default/files/boarddocuments/ 2014/2014_Library_Board_Meeting_Minutes/minutes140121.pdf.

35. *Chelsea District Library Director's Report* (Chelsea, MI: Chelsea Public Library District, March 2015), http://chelseadistrictlibrary.org/sites/default/files/ boarddocuments/2015/2015_Director_Reports/director201503.pdf.

CHAPTER 6

MARKETING YOUR COLLECTION

If handled properly the library marketing of electronic resources can lead to a deeper and richer relationship with library constituents.
—Dennis Dillon, "Strategic Marketing of Electronic Resources,"
Strategic Marketing in Library and Information Science

You just spent a good deal of money and a great deal of time on creating a great digital collection you know your community will love. You built it, but will they use it? After all that work it may be tempting to step back for a while, but don't rest yet. You need a plan to let people know where to find and how to use the collection. After the first burst of interest, continue to keep the collection in the public eye. There are a number of strategies and resources you can use to market your digital collection.

WHAT IS MARKETING?

The term *marketing* was embraced by the library world in the early 1980s when libraries began to take advantage of the research and advances of businesses' marketing.[1] From a business standpoint the need is to increase awareness of their products among current and prospective consumers with the intention of increasing purchases. Libraries have similar goals; to increase awareness of the services to current library users and non-library users. You need people to first know about your product to draw them to the website or database. Marketing involves developing a strategy for promoting services by using a number of different resources. These resources could include local radio, television, newspapers, and social media.

How is this different from your outreach activities? The *Merriam-Webster Dictionary* defines outreach as "the activity or process of bringing information or services to people." Marketing is defined as "the activities that are involved in making people aware of a company's products, making sure that the products are available to be bought." An advertisement in your local newspaper about a workshop on using your new digital collection is marketing for that event. Going out to the community showing people how to access your collection is outreach.

To market your collection you will need to have a plan covering who, when, what, and how information is provided.

- **Who:** Your outreach efforts can make marketing easier by creating a network of individuals who are interested in your library's mission. Do you know who to contact at the local schools, historical societies, newspapers, and radio stations?
- **When:** Are there points before the project starts, during and after completion when you will market the collection?
- **What:** What type of information will you share?
- **How:** What are your outlets for communication?

TYPES OF MARKETING

Marketing is something which can occur before, during, and after your collection goes online. Although there are many types of marketing strategies, there are several types which are a natural fit for libraries which you can use to promote your collection. You may already be using some of these methods:

- **Word of Mouth/Social Media Marketing:** Use Facebook, Twitter, and your Friends to spread the word about your digital collection.
- **Public Relations Marketing:** Take advantage of newspapers, radio, and television.
- **Co-Marketing:** Connect to another organization, event, or individual.

WORD OF MOUTH/SOCIAL MEDIA

People will pay more attention to the traditional marketing resources such as flyer, posters, newsletters, e-mails, and social media posts if they are coming from someone they trust and in connection with an interest rather than appearing in the mail without any context. Just as information can spread at a social event, resources like Facebook are a simple, official or unofficial way for people to share information. According to a 2014 Pew Research Center survey, more than 71 percent of Americans 18 years and older use Facebook, including more than half (56 percent) of adults over the age of 65. The site is used daily by 70 percent of those surveyed.[2]

If your library has been working on outreach you already have very important resources. All of those individuals and organizations you have connected with can be a powerful tool for word-of-mouth marketing. Historical societies, genealogy groups, or other institutions may not be able to contribute financially but they can disseminate information among their members. Word of mouth can also function as a tool to keep promotion focused on a specific community or interest group. This gives the library more control over who is contacted as opposed to a general, widespread message.

Using Your Network for Word of Mouth

Eileen O'Connell, branch manager and special collections librarian with the Albuquerque/Bernalillo County Library System New Mexico has been using both social media and her partnerships to reach her audience. The library is expanding its reach by connecting with organizations with similar interests or goals who are willing to provide a link to library websites. The Albuquerque Historical Society has a link to the library's digital collections on the society's main page. Historic Albuquerque Inc. works with the library on a series of lectures titled "People Create Cities" and also provides a link to the library's website among its own resources. These historical societies send information out to their membership, which provides helpful feedback on resource guides and encourages attendance at library lectures.

At these lectures individuals can sign up for announcements of similar events. The library uses an electronic discussion list to promote future occasions and reach an audience which is most likely to be interested. Because this announcement is electronic it can easily be forwarded on by the recipient.

The library also uses traditional posters and flyers, some of which are taken by a volunteer to one of the library's partners, Oasis Albuquerque, a senior health organization. According to O'Connell this partner then "takes them into the community on our behalf."

Social Media

There are a number of social media tools being used by libraries including Facebook, Instagram, Twitter, and YouTube. These resources can be interconnected with links from one leading to the other. Facebook and Twitter can be used to post announcements, encourage interaction with collections, and obtain feedback from users.

Who are you reaching when you use social media? When you use Facebook you are connecting with the people who have "friended" your library, or if a user "shares" your post their friend will also see your message. Facebook can directly promote your digital collection through posts or subtly link people to material by grabbing their attention and providing a link. Users are actively engaged with the site, sharing or commenting on posts.[3]

YouTube is primarily a source for videos and is second in popularity to Facebook with 6 out of 10 Internet users using the site.[4] If you have a promotional video or oral histories these can be placed on YouTube. Content can be promoted through other social media services by linking to the video or by including the link in the library's catalog record.

Instagram is a photo-sharing app which includes filters to correct images. Short videos and captions can be sent to followers. Twitter is a "microblogger" which allows people to share short, 140-character messages. Images and links to other sites can be included. Both will reach people who are following your account, and those they share your image or "tweet" with. People may send photos of your event, posters, items, send comments, or add metadata in the form of a hashtag (i.e., #mylibrary).

If you have volunteers scanning or adding metadata, ask them to note compelling images or stories. These can be used for regular posts with a backlog of possible posts ready to go online when needed. These can be divided into themes for different times of the year, connecting current celebrations with historic or local events: wedding photos for Valentine's Day, picnics and parades in summer, along with recent author book signings or workshops. Facebook is also a great place for people to share their own stories. Encourage users to share their experiences and when possible link to blogs. Did your collection have a long-lost photo from someone's family? Did they help a genealogist fill in a blank or locate a previously forgotten piece of history? See if users will share the experience and show how the collection is used and affecting users.

Using Your Images to Generate Interest

The Seattle Public Library takes its Facebook page very seriously with a dedicated team to monitor the library's account. The library has a Marketing and Online Services team of ten librarians who volunteer for two years. The program manager, Kitty Ireland, provides direction for this group. Each day one member of the team monitors the various channels and posts content while another team member prepares posts for the following day. Twitter will typically have five posts, Facebook has one to three, while Pinterest and Instagram may have one post every two weeks.

The library has used its Facebook page to engage users, provide book recommendations, poll users, and connect to collections. Images catch the user's eye while text encourages patrons to "check out this 1912 picture of our Georgetown library and visit our Neighborhood History Project online to learn more about the neighborhood." A link connects the post to the history project. Another post shows an old image of a branch library along with a birthday message for the historic location. Text below the image provides a sentence about the Seattle Historical Photograph Collection. Posts like these promote use and awareness of the collections. To maintain a steady but not overwhelming stream of posts, the Social Media Team uses Google Calendars to schedule posts which can be created in advance and entered into a timeline for posting later.

Posts are accumulated through a library form where staff can submit content. Posts are intended to engage the audience and are limited to interesting articles, books, and posts about Seattle, especially history. These efforts aimed at the Seattle public are working. As of June 2015 30,000 people had "liked" the library's Facebook page.

I Saw It on YouTube

Similar to having a library event in a museum or another outside space, having a presence on a social media site can expand the reach of the library. Having a collection on YouTube is a way to reach beyond the regular library user and into another communal space. One other benefit is that the library is not required to store the files and maintain access, which can save space on the library's server. For preservation purposes it is best to keep a separate, master copy.

Using video as the format for oral histories provides more options, such as the inclusion of still images, music, and sound effects. These features can be used to give context to the stories being told and encourage deeper engagement with media.[5] By making the videos accessible through YouTube the library can monitor the number of views for each video and check comments.

The Hernando County Public Library (HCPL) in Brooksville, Florida, has its own YouTube channel for a program called Local History Live! The people interviewed have lived in the community for fifty years or longer. The videos can be located through the library catalog (DVD copies can be checked out), through the library's Local History web page, or by searching YouTube. Fifteen videos are available. These integrate additional materials with the interviews such as old images of the speaker, events, or newspaper articles that are edited into the video. The video of Fred Blackburn's interview includes an image of the doctor who delivered him, an advertisement for a Sears portable home similar to the one he grew up in (price including floor was $1,117.00), a local mine where many people had worked, his school, church, and a moonshine still. This single video has been viewed over 200 times since it was uploaded in 2013. The interview with Frasier Mountain, a resident of the community for 90 years, has had over 350 views and five "likes."

The oral history program at HCPL is managed by Theresa "Resse" Bernier and started as part of Florida 500, a statewide celebration of the history of the state. Another staff member, Brittany McGarrity, provides background research and the supplemental images. The purpose of the archive is to preserve local history. According to Shan McQuown, who edits and publishes the interviews, they are promoted on the library's Twitter, Instagram, and Facebook accounts which have direct links.[6]

PUBLIC RELATIONS MARKETING

According to the Public Relations Society of America, "public relations is a strategic communication process that builds mutually beneficial relationships between organizations and their publics."[7] With this method you take advantage of a network of contacts and resources developed through outreach activities to inform the public about your resources. It is important to develop a strategy regarding when and where to send your information and to choose the format such as press releases, public service announcements, or more in-depth coverage.

Press Releases Long and Short

Press releases are a great, basic way to let you reach out to your local newspapers, television, and radio stations. Provide your release weeks before an event if possible. A short announcement should include a title, date, location, and a short description of the event. These media outlets will often provide public service announcements (PSAs) at no cost. Longer announcements or additional information may lead to fuller coverage of your topic. There is always a chance that you can generate enough interest to result in a longer story.

Newspapers

Newspapers are an obvious tool for spreading awareness of your collection. If you are digitizing a newspaper which is still published, it is also in the paper's interest to promote its patronage or cooperation. The company will get positive publicity by connecting itself with a popular institution generally seen to be beneficent. Often newspapers will print a long press release (several paragraphs) but a story is even better. A story will engage the audience, incite curiosity, and connect on a deeper, emotional level.

Press releases for newspapers should be clearly written, include all the important information, be timely, accurate and brief. When preparing a press release make sure you cover all the basic information:

- **What:** What is being unveiled, or announced?
- **Who:** Provide information on your organization and who to contact for more information.
- **Where:** Give the URL for your collection, or if you are having an educational session, where will it be held?
- **When:** When will the service be available or the event occur?
- **Why:** Tell why your project is interesting or important.

If the information you provide is exciting it could lead to a featured article. Include an engaging image. The image may not be used in the press release but may help your story stand apart and result in a longer story.

Getting Their Story Out: A Reporter and the Library

When seeking coverage for your new collection it is helpful to already have contacts with the local newspaper. The Highland Park Public Library in Illinois had a press release published in the *Chicago Tribune* to announce that the library had won a large grant award to digitize material for inclusion in the Illinois Digital Platform.[8] A few weeks later a story appeared in the *Chicago Tribune* featuring a large image of an elderly woman and quotes from her history as an early pioneer.[9] The beginning of the article focused on the woman, whose strong gaze in the picture makes the reader curious about the rest of her story. This is not just a nameless woman in an old photo. This is Emilia Nafe, a women who spent weeks on a boat to come to America and once here survived hard winters. She is a person whose life experiences are familiar yet different enough to be interesting.

Greg Trotter, local beat reporter for the *Chicago Tribune*, saw the release and realized the potential for a longer piece. He spoke to individuals at the library and the historical society to learn more about the project and why it was important to digitize this material. In an effort to find some examples to make the story more engaging, he asked to see the interviews of the first settlers to Highland Park. As Totter dug into the transcripts he found that Emilia Nafe and her story read "like a novel." The story of her life became the focal point for the article.

Trotter is "always more interested in a story if I get it directly" instead of through a mass news release sent to many other reporters. His advice for libraries who would like to have this level of newspaper coverage is to develop a relationship with the local reporters who cover the library or similar institutions. Let them know when you may have a story. Although press releases are useful for getting information out widely, reporters will be more interested in unique stories that will not be covered by others.

This story was an exception in that the press release led Totter to investigate further. Because Totter regularly covers library events and programs ranging from lending ukuleles to new archival material, he pays attention to the releases. The library's public relations office normally contacts him if there is a story, but because of his relationship with the library he noticed the release and was curious to learn more.

If you are unsure who to contact at your local newspaper, try searching their stories and see if there is an individual who tends to cover the library, historical societies, or your community in general. Send information directly to this person and you may develop a mutually beneficial relationship.

Radio

Just as newspapers are limited to inches of space for your public service announcement, your local radio stations are limited to minutes or seconds. If your radio station has a limit on the length of the PSA, make sure your announcement is the correct length. Focus on the goal of your message, and if possible try to make the PSA personally relatable.

Roundup's Inside Man on the Radio

Dale Alger is another librarian who wears many hats. He is the school librarian and director of the Roundup Community Library and is vice president of the Musselshell Historical Museum in Roundup, Montana. When there was an opportunity for the community to get a grant to participate in the Montana Memory Project there were several collections they could draw from, including a rich collection of photographs at the museum.

Promoting the collection meant press releases to the two local papers and working with the radio station, which proved to be easy since Alger was already broadcasting on KLMB, 88.1 FM, Panther Country Radio on Tuesday mornings. Normally he talks about sports, the local museum, library, and events at the public schools. For a few weeks Alger could be heard talking about the Montana Memory Project and how the images could be accessed. The station reaches not only the local community of Roundup, but also four other towns and portions of Billings, the largest city in Montana.

CO-MARKETING

Working with other organizations to market your collection can help your library reach a wider audience. These organizations and the people associated with them can be drawn in by a subject or someone famous who already has a following. Your library can take advantage of the other organization's brand and name recognition. A known name can help your event, your library, or project stand apart from others and draw attention. Attaching a project to an author or celebrity (past or present) can help to generate interest in your collection. The Oak Park Public Library in Illinois has Hacking Hemingway: Cracking the Code to the Vault, and with that name comes the reputation of the author and a community of scholars and fans of author Ernest Hemingway.

In 2005 the Oak Park Public Library announced it had obtained a state library grant for $86,900 for Hacking Hemingway.[10] The project had only just been funded but its name and subject matter were enough to generate early interest. On Facebook the Friends of the Oak Park Public Library posted a congratulatory message with the olive green logo for the project. The logo includes the project title with the first two words in a 1920s-inspired font under the author's bearded image. The *Chicago Tribune* published a story about the project and the library's Twitter account provided a link to a press release at OakPark.com. The project has the benefit of having name recognition and a collection which will draw interest based on the fact that Hemingway is a famous author associated with a specific time, writing style, and adventurous life.

How do you take an example where marketing is greatly aided by an already popular subject and turn it into something that will work for your collection? The efforts at Oak Park will be successful because many of the resources were obvious; audience, support networks, and a compelling story. With Heming-way there is already an audience and community connections in the form of societies which were established and willing to share information throughout their own networks.

But you don't need a famous collection to take advantage of the same tools. Connecting with another organization or tying a collection to an author can help draw people to your digital collection. If your community has been the home of a famous individual, you may have an image of their home in your collection. If your library participates in the National Endowment for the Arts' Big Read you can use that large event and theme to connect people with your collections.

CASE STUDY

SOCIAL MEDIA, PUBLIC RELATIONS AND CO-MARKETING

Never limit yourself to one type of marketing. Depending on your goals and situation, find the method which will work best for your project. The Gail Borden Public Library District in Elgin, Illinois, has used several methods to promote different aspects of the collection and resources, including a network of contacts. Although the library has the benefit of a dedicated marketing team, many of the tools they are using are available to most libraries. The library serves an area population of 144,597 with one branch, 27 librarians, and 90 other staff. They circulate almost one million children's books each year. Over 33,000 children attend their programs annually. Total circulation of materials is well over two million.[11] They are obviously not having any trouble reaching out to the community and this has been reflected by some of the many awards the library has received.

The Gail Borden Public Library District is accustomed to receiving accolades. The library was voted the Library of the Year in 2006 by the North Suburban Library System and the same year received the Marshall Cavendish Award for Excellence in Library Programing from the American Library Association.[12] In 2009 the library was awarded the Elgin Image award for their veterans' history project and the National Medal for Museum and Library Service for their efforts to "reach out to people of all ages and backgrounds and invite them to explore our wonderfully diverse history, culture, and literature."[13] The library received international recognition in 2010 when it received second place in the eighth annual International Federation of Library Associations and Institutions' International Marketing Award for the program: StoryTubes: Kids Go Live with Books.[14]

Social Media

The StoryTubes program and contest encouraged children to create a two-minute promotional video for their favorite book. This effort promoted the library, generated content, encouraged engagement, and contained learning components.[15] StoryTubes was an effort which ultimately reached children in four countries and was copied by libraries around the world. This project used social media and the heartfelt enthusiasm of readers to spread interest in the library and reading in general. By creating easily shared videos on YouTube the children who created the content were able to share their videos with peers. Teachers promoted the project in the classroom and viewers could vote on their favorite video.

This effort became so popular that a search of YouTube results in over 10,000 results for StoryTube. When a marketing effort is shared by others online it can get widespread attention and the promotion is out of the hands of the library. There is a greater awareness of the institution, but you may find yourself with more interest than you can handle. This can be prevented through mindful marketing and utilizing the networks created through outreach to manage a word-of-mouth campaign.

Public Relations and Word of Mouth

The Gail Borden Public Library leverages both formal partnerships and personal connections to assist with word-of-mouth and public relations promotion. Melissa Lane, manager of local history and digital preservation, prefers to reach out to specific partners for content and promotion. For a number of years the library has worked to expand its reach beyond the walls of the library. This has involved connecting with and promoting events at other institutions. Art galleries, schools, museums, historical societies, the city of Elgin, and others are working with the library, hosting exhibits and events. By reaching out to these partners the library is able to augment its reach and potential market.

Knowing who to work with on a marketing project can be an important tool. The library administration understands this and each year compiles a list of library staff who are members of different organizations such as Kiwanis, Lions Club, and other societies. According to Lane, the library administration maintains a list of contacts with high-level individuals through a network library staff, but many of the marketing efforts are realized through lower levels of organizations. Lane is also the teen outreach librarian and has connections with teachers, school staff, and committees. She has "people I can call on at those locations that will help me market the programs because they are dear to that specific audience." These connections have led to school trips to the library for different events. By knowing who to contact within the library for different events, the library is able to reach out to specific audiences who are interested and supportive of the subject matter.

The library has a team of four to five individuals who work to promote library events and collections. There is a twenty-page newsletters published every two months which lists book clubs, oral history projects, exhibits, and the many other events. There are so many different programs happening at this library that there is some friendly competition between departments to have an event listed. An online event calendar and the library Facebook page are also used to promote activities. By associating with other like-minded groups and individuals, the marketing materials developed by the library have a higher impact and greater reach than if the library was operating without this carefully developed network.

Just as the library hopes to take advantage of the opportunities that result from working with other organizations, those institutions benefit from working with the library. The library hosted the Big Read and the library newsletter is filled with events at the partner institutions. A 2015 event, Reflections: Flowing through Time, is expected to have 15–20 partners.[16] The website for this project contains historic images, including one from the library's collection of digitized postcards. Events listed include a cemetery tour to benefit the Elgin Historical Museum, an architectural tour by the North East Neighborhood Association tour, and a sky show and history lecture at the local planetarium. These events are included in the library newsletter and includes the logos of the partner institutions.

The networks the library has developed as part of its outreach efforts have proven to be a useful resource for word-of-mouth marketing. Lane feels that the majority of direct marketing (flyers and mailers) are ignored but "if you can make a connection and have a conversation with the person, they are going to be more likely to want to find out more about what you are trying to archive or they could work together with you." Lane lives and works in Elgin. Her children went through the schools and she knows teachers, principals, and school librarians. Even living in a large community she sees many familiar faces and has opportunities to share information about library projects.

A Name You Can Trust

Two very specific digital collections drew inspiration and promotion from the 2013 Big Read and Tim O'Brien's *The Things They Carried*. The Big Read is an annual event sponsored by the National Endowment for the Arts to promote reading. Communities which participate are provided with training, educational and promotional materials, and benefit by being associated with a national event.[17] This event series started in 2007 and has been very successful. A collection associated with the event will benefit from being connected to both the Big Read (a large and well-organized event associated with literacy, education, and community) and a chosen book.

For the celebration in Elgin there were over forty partners for this event, including several veterans organizations, the local police and fire departments, school district, university, community college, and several businesses. This was a large celebration with many components, one of which was a collection of images of local Vietnam veterans, some carrying objects they had with them during the war and others carrying scars. This series of images was directly connected to the subject matter of the Tim O'Brien book. Local veterans were contacted for participation. Marketing was linked to the larger event and took advantage of interest in the Big Read, the marketing resources for that program, and the partners.

That same year the theme of items carried by individuals was expanded to the Hispanic Heritage Month Celebration. To find participants for the project and to encourage promotion, there was a specific individual in the library who had the professional and personal connections needed. Christina Viglucci, the Hispanic services coordinator, used her personal connections and Facebook to find local individuals who would share items representing their lives and links to their Latin American roots. As a member of the Elgin Hispanic Network she knew who to contact. Viglucci is responsible for Spanish translations of resources on the library website and made sure that the collection for Hispanic Heritage Month was available in Spanish.

Just as many libraries have used partners to aid in scanning and hosting material, and have reached out to their communities for content, marketing does not need to be a solo activity. The work you have already accomplished with outreach can be leveraged for mutual marketing activities to promote your collections. ▦■■

Chapter Synopsis

Libraries can play to their strength as community centers and their connections with schools, businesses, and other like-minded institutions to reach a wider audience.

- Word of mouth is a powerful tool to promote your collections.
- Social media should be used consistently, but posting too often could overwhelm users.

- Take advantage of the interconnectivity between different social media platforms to save time.
- Social media posts can be handled by a small team.
- Having a carefully selected list of contacts will help you keep your message on track and connect you to different segments of your community.
- Partner with other organizations in your community and promote each other's programs and events.
- Take advantage of name recognition.
- Use multiple forms of marketing to reach library and non-library users.

NOTES

1. Elizabeth J. Wood, "Strategic Planning and the Marketing Process: Library Applications," *Journal of Academic Librarianship* 9, no. 1 (1983): 15–20; Alan R. Andreasen, "Advancing Library Marketing," *Journal of Library Administration*, 1 no. 3 (1981): 17–32.

2. Maeve Duggan et al., "Social Media Update 2014," Pew Research Center website, January 2015, www.pewinternet.org/2015/01/09/social-media-update-2014/.

3. Maeve Duggan et al., "Frequency of Social Media Use," Pew Research Center website, www.pewinternet.org/2015/01/09/frequency-of-social-media-use-2/.

4. Monica Anderson, "5 Facts about Online Video, For YouTube's 10th Birthday," Pew Research Center website (February 12, 2015), www.pewresearch.org/fact-tank/2015/02/12/5-facts-about-online-video-for-youtubes-10th-birthday/.

5. Peter Kaufman, "Oral History in the Video Age," *Oral History Review* 40, no. 1 (2013): 1–7, doi: 10.1093/ohr/oht033.

6. "Pay It Forward: Hernando County's Local History Live Program," Tampa Bay Library Consortium website (March 7, 2014), http://tblc.org/events/pay-it-forward -hernando-county-oral-history.

7. "What Is Public Relations?" Public Relations Society of America website, www.prsa .org/aboutprsa/publicrelationsdefined/#.VV4LevlVo.

8. Highland Park Public Library, "From the Community: Highland Park History Going Digital," *Chicago Tribune* (January 16, 2015), www.chicagotribune.com/suburbs/highland-park/community/chi-ugc-article-highland-park-history-going -digital-2015-01-16-story.html.

9. Greg Trotter, "Historical Tale among Artifacts to Be Digitally Preserved," *Chicago Tribune* (February 3, 2015), www.chicagotribune.com/suburbs/highland-park/news/ct-highland-park-historical-archives-lk-tl-20150130-story.html.

10. Jodi Kolo, "Library awarded $86,900 grant to Digitize Historical Ernest Hemingway Archives," Oak Park Public Library, Janary 18, 2015, http://oppl.org/about/library -news/library-awarded-86900-grant-digitize-historical-ernest-hemingway-archives.

11. *Public Libraries Survey, Fiscal Year 2012* (Washington, DC: Institute of Museum and Library Services, 2012).

12. "Gail Borden Library Voted 2006 Library of the Year," Gail Borden Public Library District website (2006), www.gailborden.info/about-the-library/history-of-the -library/244-2006-library-of-the-year.

13. "Gail Borden Library Wins Nation's Highest Library Honor," Gail Borden Public Library District website (2009), www.gailborden.info/about-the-library/ history-of-the-library/930-gail-borden-library-wins-nations-highest-library-honor.

14. Christie Koontz, "Excellence in Marketing: 2002–2012," in *Marketing Library and Information Services II: A Global Outlook* (The Hague, Netherlands: International Federation of Library Associations Publications, 2013).

15. Faith Brautigam and Denise Raleigh, *Marketing Library and Information Services II: A Global Outlook* (The Hague, Netherlands: International Federation of Library Associations Publications, 2013).

16. "Reflections: Flowing Through Time," Gail Borden Library website, www.gailborden .info/library-info/1878-reflections.

17. "About," National Endowment for the Arts website, www.neabigread.org/about.php.

CHAPTER 7

DIGITAL PRESERVATION

I think everyone who has worked on this has that visceral feeling of we've got to protect this, we have to get this on someone's dark archive, we've got to get this preserved.

—Palin Bree, library manager, Boyce Ditto Public Library, Texas

W hether the impetus for digitization was a need to limit the physical handling of fragile materials, to increase access to a valuable collection, or some combination of both, the outputs of any digitization project include a set of digital files and associated descriptive information about those files. Combined together these digital files and metadata constitute a set of digital objects that a library is now responsible for managing.

GENERAL CONCEPTS

It is important to recognize that digitization is not the final act in preserving a collection of materials, but instead should be considered the first of many ongoing activities that characterize digital preservation. Digital preservation has been defined as "the series of managed activities necessary to ensure continued access to digital materials for as long as necessary."[1] It is the continuous and active management qualities of digital preservation work that distinguish it from analog preservation activities. This contrast is directly related to the difference between the nature of analog and digital information.

Simply put, digital information is more dependent on a variety of elements to allow it to be viewed and understood by humans. To access, view, and understand the information within a photograph or letter that is sitting in a box at a given library, a person only needs to open the box and take out the item. Once converted from analog to digital form, the digital version of that same photograph now requires additional technological elements, including computer hardware and software, to render the digital file and make it viewable and understandable by human beings. This dependence on digital technology is the inherent challenge confronting those seeking to provide continued access to digital information. Increasingly rapid technological changes cause digital hardware, software, and file formats to quickly become outdated and obsolete. Analog preservation strategies, such as placing materials in stable housing to slow decay and degradation, do not apply to digital objects. Instead, active management of digital objects is required, responding to technological changes by continuously moving and migrating digital information to ensure current and future access.

Within the primary digital preservation goal of ensuring long-term access to digital objects, there are a series of concepts and related activities outlined by Caplan that provide insight into additional goals of digital preservation.[2]

Availability

In order to preserve and continue to provide access to digital objects a library must have control over those objects. For libraries engaging in digitization projects, depending on whether digitization was performed in-house or by a vendor, the resulting digital objects should be regularly available to perform additional preservation activities and provide access to them.

Identity

At a bare minimum, a digital object should be assigned a unique, persistent identifier to distinguish it from other digital objects. Additional descriptive information created during or after digitization supports long-term preservation and access by providing context and increasing discoverability.

Understandability

Similar to the goal of identity, digital objects should contain all the information needed to be understood by those who discover those digital objects in the future. This might include references to documentation such as an archival finding aid for a collection of items that were digitized, or technical metadata related to digital images.

Fixity

An additional goal of digital preservation is ensuring that digital objects are protected from unauthorized changes. Fixity refers to a set of activities that include regular checking of the integrity of digital objects to ensure they haven't changed, usually by utilizing checksums. Checksums function like a digital fingerprint for a file and can be compared against the file over time to determine if the file has been altered.

Authenticity

Digital objects are especially vulnerable to change and manipulation. Maintaining the authenticity of a digital object entails ensuring that "the digital material is what it purports to be," or in other words, "the integrity of both the source and the content of an object can be verified."[3] Activities related to maintaining authenticity include developing and implementing policies and procedures that outline how digital objects are to be protected against unauthorized changes, as well as documentation in the form of preservation metadata that records authorized changes, such as migration to a new file format.

Viability

Viability refers to "the quality of being readable from media."[4] The fragility and ephemerality of digital media require constant vigilance to ensure that the data stored on digital media hardware continues to be available. Regularly refreshing media hardware by moving copies of data to contemporary media, as well as storing multiple copies of data on multiple media devices, are important strategies in actively managing digital objects over the long term.

Renderability

As mentioned previously, hardware and software obsolescence is one of the biggest challenges faced by those seeking to preserve digital objects. Digital objects are dependent on the relationship of file formats to hardware and software environments to be able to be rendered, viewed, and used. The two most prominent strategies for meeting the digital preservation goal of renderability are migration and emulation.

The above concepts represent a number of the high-level goals that drive the underlying notion of active management within digital preservation. It is important to recognize that the organization that has taken responsibility for the long-term management of its digital objects may not necessarily implement all of the activities listed above to ensure these digital preservation goals continue to be achieved. At the same time an overall understanding of the purpose and functions of digital preservation is important when making decisions about how to go about managing and providing access to digital objects into the future.

STANDARDS

Just as there are standards and best practices that guide the efforts of libraries in digitization projects, so are there standards that assist in efforts to ensure long-term preservation and access to the digital objects that result from digitization activities. An awareness and basic understanding of these standards is important, even if a library organization is not planning on developing and implementing a comprehensive in-house digital preservation program.

OAIS

The Open Archival Information System reference model, otherwise known as OAIS, is the primary foundational digital preservation standard. Originating out of the Consultative Committee for Space Data Systems, which sought to develop formal standards for the long-term storage of data generated during space missions, OAIS "has become a foundation resource for understanding digital preservation, a language for talking about digital preservation issues, and a starting point for implementing digital preservation solutions."[5] To be OAIS-compliant, an archive must implement the six functional entities that outline the OAIS archive's preservation and access operations, including ingest, archival storage, data management, preservation planning, access, and administration.

The OAIS standards utilize the concept of an "information package" to describe the entity that is the focus of preservation and access. An information package "consists of the object that is the focus of preservation, along with metadata necessary to support its long-term preservation, access, and understandability."[6] An information package could include just a single digital file and its associated metadata, or all the digital files and metadata resulting from a digitization project. OAIS functions as a conceptual framework and therefore is not proscriptive in how the functions it outlines should be implemented. In fact, it is common for different parts of an OAIS archive to be implemented via different software and hardware environments, or even across multiple organizations. When determining options for digital preservation solutions, a library organization should investigate and understand if and how a vendor or service provider conforms to the OAIS standard as a basic starting point for ensuring long-term access to its digital content.

STRATEGIES

As stated briefly above, digital preservation does not start at the end of a digitization project, but rather preservation actions should be built into the process from the beginning to ensure the opportunity for long-term access of the digital objects produced during digitization activities.

Digitization

Capture, or the process of converting an item from analog to digital format, is a key step that has implications for the long-term viability of digital objects. There are numerous resources outlining standards and best practices to guide the conversion process, ensuring the resulting digital objects authentically represent the information and characteristics of the original analog material.

The selection of file formats that the newly converted digital information will be encoded into is a foundational digital preservation action during the digitization process. File formats should be selected with an eye towards long-term access and use, and should include characteristics such as being uncompressed, well-supported by current software, non-proprietary, and based on open specifications. There are many current standard preservation file formats for common types of content that should be considered when designing digitization workflows to support long-term access of digital content.

Additionally, a digital file is dependent upon various forms of metadata that allow it to be discovered, rendered, and used into the future. The generation and management of metadata is key to the long-term access of digital objects, and is another fundamental preservation activity that occurs during digitization. Decisions about the creation and management of descriptive, technical, administrative, and structural metadata will have significant implications for the ability to preserve and provide access to digitized materials. Happily, there are many resources providing guidance to assist in metadata decisions related to specific types of content.

The details of the design, development, and implementation of digitization workflows will have a significant impact on the continued efforts to preserve and provide access to the resulting digital objects and should be considered carefully and thoughtfully, with reference to existing standards and best practices, to integrate preservation actions throughout the digitization process.

Archival Storage

In OAIS terms, archival storage is "the portion of the archival system that manages the long-term storage and maintenance of digital materials entrusted to the OAIS."[7] An important defining function of archival storage is to ensure that "the bit streams comprising the preserved information remain complete and renderable over the long term."[8] This primary function distinguishes archival storage from other common forms of storage, most often understood as backups. Backing up copies of digital files to multiple storage media or storage environments is an important part of any digital preservation strategy, but only creating and storing additional copies does not constitute archival storage. Instead, archival storage includes regular monitoring and integrity checking of the digital objects being stored to ensure no unauthorized changes have occurred to those digital objects.

An illustration may help here. Imagine a scenario where a particular digital image file is changed due to corruption caused by a storage media hardware failure. Parts of the information within the digital image might be lost, so for example where there should be an image of a mountain, there may now only be lines of color. The storage media hardware could have failed due to age or environmental conditions, such as not being cooled properly. Even if eventually new copies of this file are produced and stored on new hardware, the corrupted image file will continue to exist and may not be discovered until access and use are attempted at a future date. Regular fixity checking performed on digital files in archival storage ensures that any changes to files are immediately recognized and steps can then be taken to repair, restore, or replace a particular file from additional copies stored on other storage media. Additionally, archival storage should include strategies such as storage media hardware refreshment and replacement, as well as geographic distribution of copies of digital objects to mitigate against loss incurred as a result of multiple forms of disaster.

Preservation Planning

As outlined previously, simply maintaining digital objects in their current state and original formats is not enough to ensure long-term preservation and access. Technological changes will continue to occur and even today's preservation file formats are likely to face obsolescence in the future. Planning and strategizing for these eventual changes is a critical component of digital preservation activities. Stated simply, "determining which preservation strategies will be developed and when and in what circumstance the strategies will be implemented is the essence of digital preservation."[9] In other words, preservation planning is a core activity within any digital preservation endeavor. There are numerous preservation strategies that have been proposed and are being pursued to overcome the challenges of software, hardware, and file format obsolescence.[10] Two of the most prominent strategies are migration and emulation.

Migration entails transferring and transforming the content of digital objects from one file format to another with a goal to "preserve the intellectual content of digital objects and to retain the ability for clients to retrieve, display, and otherwise use them in the face of constantly changing technology."[11] Pursuing migration as a preservation strategy does include the risk of the potential loss of "significant characteristics" of the digital objects because newer formats, software, and hardware environments may not be able to render and support all of the functions and features of the original content.

Emulation includes utilizing a combination of software and hardware to reproduce a specific computing environment within a different, often newer, system. An example would be an emulator that would allow users to open and use files originally created on MS-DOS, an early text-based personal computing operating system, long since replaced by more visually oriented systems. By focusing on reproducing the original computing environment needed to render, view, and interact with specific file formats, emulation attempts to overcome technological obsolescence without having to change the file formats directly. Until fairly recently, the costs and level of complexity associated with emulation resulted in limited adoption as a preservation strategy, but some recent projects have demonstrated the viability of emulation as an approach for achieving the long-term preservation and access of digital objects.

Planning for and developing strategies to cope with technological change is not something that a single library should consider as its' sole responsibility. Instead, the development, implementation, and monitoring of preservation strategies is a collaborative endeavor shared by libraries, archives, and museums and should be pursued with collective interests in mind.

OPTIONS AND TOOLS

When considering options to implement strategies to support long-term preservation and access of digital objects, decisions around selecting in-house
vs. outsourced options are somewhat similar to those encountered during
planning for digitization. Currently, there is not a single software solution or
service that will provide functionality and support for all digital preservation
activities. Instead, there are a variety of tools of various shapes and sizes available that perform specific digital preservation activities. Increasingly, these
discrete software tools have been combined into larger software packages
and services that offer enhanced digital preservation functionality. While the
advances in software tools and services supporting digital preservation have
increased in recent years, it is important to recognize that these technological
solutions are subject to the same risk of change and obsolescence as the digital
objects they have been designed to assist in preserving over time. Therefore, it
is important to evaluate and assess digital preservation tools with a perspective
that initial decisions around tool or service implementation are likely to be
revisited in the near future.

As both open source and commercial digital preservation software tools
and services have advanced and matured, there are now multiple options for
organizations both large and small to get started with their own digital preservation endeavors. Additionally, with more institutions establishing digital
preservation programs there are increasing models, case studies, and information about software and service options available for smaller organizations
to review and consider in their decision-making process.

BEYOND TECHNOLOGY

It is equally important to understand that digital preservation is not merely a
technological issue that will be solved with technological solutions, but should
be seen as a balance between an organizational infrastructure, technological
infrastructure, and a resources framework, as articulated by the "three-legged
stool" analogy provided by the Digital Preservation Management Tutorial.[12]
Just as organization-wide planning was likely involved in the development of
a digitization project or program, so should digital preservation be seen as an
organization-wide responsibility and commitment.

Granular decisions about software tools or services are likely to change,
but the decision to commit to preserve digital content over the long term is
substantial and is strengthened through codification in the form of policies
and procedures documents. The creation of high-level policy documents solid-
ifies an organization's mandate, purpose, and goals for digital preservation,

and procedures documents outline at a lower level how the organization will go about achieving those goals. Policy documents can be used to bolster the argument and case for allocating resources for digital preservation, especially if they clearly articulate the need for digital preservation and connect this to an organization's overall mission and goals. Not every organization may need to develop their own digital preservation policy materials, particularly those that are part of a collaborative network with its own policy framework, but the value of producing and maintaining these organizational documents is fundamental to the sustainability of any digital preservation endeavor.

Most fundamental to the sustainability of any digital preservation program is the ongoing commitment of resources to support continued access to digital objects of enduring value. The costs of digital preservation can range from in-house staffing with digital preservation responsibilities to annual subscription fees for cloud-based archival storage. The resources arena highlights one of the distinctions between the act of digitization and ongoing management of the resulting digital objects. Whereas digitization is often a one-time activity with one-time costs, ensuring ongoing access to digital objects requires the ongoing commitment of resources to support continued digital preservation efforts. While there are growing opportunities for cost savings for digital preservation activities by joining collaborative networks, such as state memory projects, some amount of resources will likely be required on a regular basis to provide continued access to an organization's digital collections.[13] There are emerging cost models that provide templates for attempting to estimate ongoing costs related to digital preservation, but even considering and planning for near-term costs during the development of digitization projects can put an organization at an advantage, especially if these costs are built into external funding proposals.

With more and more libraries, archives, and museums of all sizes creating and acquiring digital content on a regular basis, the wealth of materials now widely available to the public positions cultural heritage institutions at the forefront of the production of new knowledge. It is important to keep in mind that while potentially more complex than previous preservation activities, digital preservation represents the latest effort of libraries, archives, museums, and similar institutions in their valuable and critical role as stewards of the cultural record.

TAKING ACTION NOW

In light of the information presented above, developing and implementing a successful digital preservation program may only seem feasible for large institutions with a large amount of resources, but even the smallest organization can take steps to ensure that its digital objects remain available into the future. First and foremost, digital preservation is a collaborative effort, and no one organization is likely to achieve all elements of a successful program by itself. One of the most important elements is understanding the importance of building partnerships and establishing collaborations with other organizations of various sizes and shapes. Investigating and possibly joining a statewide, regional, or even national consortium of libraries, archives, and museums to coordinate digital preservation activities and sharing costs is one of the first activities a smaller organization should consider. As mentioned above, there are many state libraries that organize and offer services around storage and access to digitized content from smaller libraries and historical societies. Beyond building relationships there are some additional steps outlined below that will assist in the management of digital content in the near term:

- **Create an inventory of digital content:** Gaining basic administrative and intellectual control over digital objects will assist in future decision-making around the near-term and long-term preservation of those objects, including decisions concerning storage options.
- **Perform selection and appraisal:** Not all digital content may have long-term, enduring value. Incorporating the determination of priorities around what digital objects should be kept for the long term will be very important, especially in a limited resource environment.
- **Implement basic archival storage:** Storing multiple copies of digital objects, along with checksums to verify authenticity, even for the immediate near future will assist in mitigating against loss. Outside of the option of storing content in a networked storage environment, selecting stable storage media such as multiple external hard drives or RAID arrays are better current choices than increasingly obsolete storage media such as CDs or DVDs.[14] Attempting to store multiple copies in multiple locations through a cloud storage service option is another increasingly affordable option.

CASE STUDY

COLLECTIONS BUILT AND LOST AND BUILT AGAIN

Quincy, Illinois, was founded when in 1822 the area was settled by John Wood, a veteran of the War of 1812.[15] This city of 40,633 situated on high limestone bluffs overlooking the Mississippi River is known for its "architecturally and historically significant structures" and arts programs.[16] The Quincy Public Library, which dates back to 1841, circulates over 600,000 items each year and has a budget of over $2 million.[17]

The Quincy Public Library started digitizing in 1998 as part of the Alliance Library System (ALS). With funding from an IMLS Leadership grant, libraries in the ALS were able to purchase equipment, learn about the digitization process, and add their collections to a larger site titled Early Illinois Women and Other Unsung Heroes. Libraries contributed information on first ladies, educators, doctors, and pioneers from the first 100 years of Illinois statehood (1818–1918). The site launched in 1999 and is hosted by Bradley University.[18] When the library started working on this project it was a learning process. The Quincy Public Library did not have a plan or really considered preservation because the goal was to make information about little-known but important women in the history of Illinois available. Early Illinois Women met that goal.

With their first successful project launched, the ALS took on another collection in 1999: Illinois Alive; The Heritage and Texture of a Pivotal State during the First Century of Statehood. This was a totally separate project with twenty-six libraries contributing content, including Quincy. According to Iris Nelson, reference and local history librarian at Quincy, the site held information on authors, African Americans, women, immigration, businesses, and had a timeline with links to other history sites. There were tools for educators, class exercises in Playing Detective with Documents, Emotional Autobiographies, and Education of Women. At the Quincy Library there were programs to promote the new website.

The Quincy Public Library and the ALS continued to work on new collections; the next was Early Heroes and Heroines of Illinois History: An Interactive Multimedia Memory Montage, also called 4M. This site launched in 2004, was completed in 2005, and was nominated in 2006 by Museums and the Web, an "international conference for culture and heritage online," for Best of the Web in the category of online exhibitions.[19] Partners on this site included the ALS, the Mid-Illinois Talking Book Center, and the Illinois State Talking Book and Braille Service. The site had a warm brown background complementing the sepia-tone images and included movies, books with flipable pages, and audio descriptions of the images for the visually impaired. The site featured seven individuals.[20] For each person there were links to their images, articles about their lives, and in some cases there were journal entries using FlipBook or movies. This site appears to have been taken down by April 2009.

Two of the original collections, Early Heroes and Illinois Alive, are gone. What happened? It was not the fault of the Quincy Public Library that the websites are no longer available. The merger of the library systems was not foreseen. The files were moved before the library system's merger and much of the content was transitioned to the Illinois Digital Archive.

The Alliance Library System was created in 1993 through a merger of four other systems and in 1998 was one of twelve regional library systems in Illinois. Funded by the Illinois State Library, it served about 300 libraries ranging from small special libraries to large academic ones and provided educational opportunities, library development, and many other services. In 2011 the system merged with four other systems to form the Reaching Across Illinois Library System (RAILS).[21] Other mergers that year reduced ten library systems to just three, Chicago, Illinois Heartland, and RAILS.[22] Somewhere among those shifts in the association the websites for the ALS collections were lost. Although these sites are no longer active in their original form, some of the pages can still be accessed through the Internet Archive's Wayback Machine.[23] Many of the images from these collections were added to the Illinois Digital Archive (IDA) under the title Illinois Alive! Early Heroes and Heroines. This collection contains forty-six items, primarily images. The FlipBooks, audio files, and movies are not in the IDA.

The Quincy Library does not have any great regrets about the loss of the two websites. Both provided a learning experience, and they provided users with resources and increased awareness of the library's collections. Although Nelson may wish there was still electronic access to a dissertation on Lincoln, the paper copy is still available at the library.

As part of the digitization process the library kept copies of the files on Zip drives. Those drives are still at the library and could possibly be added to a digital collection in the future. When the collection was scanned these drives were a common form of storage for electronic files. The library does not have the software required to access these files but may be able to run an emulation program to retrieve the images. This example highlights the importance of regularly refreshing storage media to ensure digital collections are being stored on stable contemporary storage media to limit the potential complexity of recovering and providing access to the files.

Some aspects of the original website may be lost. The books with turning pages which were part of Illinois Alive were made possible by using a proprietary software called FlipBook. Users were required to download this software to view the files. It is unknown if those files could be opened with the current form of the software. This is an instance where the viability and renderability of the files is in question. It may be possible to find a copy of a software on an older computer or get the software to work on a modern computer by installing a system which functions in the same manner. This would require the library or the manufacturer to have copies of the software and the programs to run.

Digitization is a learning process. In 2008 the library received an LSTA grant funds for the Quincy Area Historic Photo Collection. This collection contains 3,828 images from a local collector and is available through the Illinois Digital Archive.[24] Copies of the image files are kept by the library as both JPEG and TIFF files on the library's network and external hard drives. ▪■▪

Chapter Synopsis

- Digital preservation is a *series of managed activities* necessary to ensure continued access to digital materials.
- Standards, specifically the Open Archival Information System reference model, outline the elements needed to develop and implement a sustainable digital preservation program.
- Backing up digital files *does not equal* archival storage.
- Currently, there is not a single digital preservation software solution, and today's tools are likely to be replaced by new tools in the near future.

Digital preservation is not merely a technological issue that will be solved with technological solutions, but should be seen as a *balance between an organizational infrastructure, technological infrastructure, and a resources framework.*

NOTES

1. Neil Beagrie, M. Jones, and Digital Preservation Coalition, *Preservation Management of Digital Materials: The Handbook* (London: Digital Preservation Coalition, 2002).
2. Priscilla Caplan, "The Preservation of Digital Materials," *Library Technology Reports* 44, no. 2 (2008): 8.
3. Priscilla Caplan, "Digital Preservation Handbook," Digital Preservation Coalition website, www.dpconline.org/advice/preservationhandbook; Caplan, "Preservation of Digital Materials," 8.
4. Priscilla Caplan, "The Preservation of Digital Materials," 8.
5. Brian Lavoie, *Technology Watch Report: The Open Archival Information System Reference Model: Introductory Guide* (Dublin, OH: Online Computer Library Center, 2014): 8. doi: http://dx.doi.org/10.7207/twr14-02.
6. Ibid.
7. Lavoie, *Technology Watch Report*, 12.
8. Ibid.
9. Nancy McGovern et al., "Preservation Planning," Digital Preservation Management, Implementing Short-Term Strategies for Long-Term Problems, tutorial, 2012, www.dpworkshop.org/dpm-eng/foundation/oais/preservation.html.

10. Ibid.

11. Priscilla Caplan, Digital Preservation Coalition Handbook, (2002).

12. "Introduction," Digital Preservation Management website, www.dpworkshop.org/dpm-eng/program/index.html.

13. "State Digital Resources: Memory Projects, Online Encyclopedias, Historical & Cultural Materials Collections," Library of Congress website, https://www.loc.gov/rr/program/bib/statememory/.

14. "Store: Storage Media and Hardware," Activists' Guide to Archiving Video website (2013), http://archiveguide.witness.org/store/storage-media-hardware.

15. "Community Overview," City of Quincy, Illinois website, www.ci.quincy.il.us/government/CityDepartments/PD/community-profile/overview.

16. "Honors & Awards," City of Quincy, Illinois website, www.ci.quincy.il.us/government/CityDepartments/PD/community-profile/honors.

17. *Quincy Public Library: Public Libraries Survey, Fiscal Year 2012* (Washington, DC: Institute of Museum and Library Services, 2012).

18. Early Illinois Women & Other Unsung Heroes website, www.bulibstats.net/illinoiswomen.

19. "Best of the Web: Nominees," Museums and the Web 2006 website, www.archimuse.com/mw2006/best/list.html.

20. "Early Heroes and Heroines of Illinois History: An Interactive Multimedia Memory Montage," Wayback Machine website, https://web.archive.org/web/20080705025204/www.illinoisalive.info/main.htm.

21. Michael Kelley, "Merger of Illinois System Nears Completion," *Library Journal* 136, no. 8 (2011).

22. "Historical Timeline," Illinois State Library website, www.cyberdriveillinois.com/departments/library/about/library-history-timeline.html.

23. "Illinois Alive! The Heritage and Texture of a Pivotal State during the First Century of Statehood (1818–1918)," Wayback Machine website, https://web.archive.org/web/20011205232543/www.alliancelibrarysystem.com/Projects/IllinoisAlive/index.html.

24. "Quincy Area Historic Photo Collection," Illinois Digital Archive website, www.idaillinois.org/cdm/search/collection/qpl.

RESOURCES

COPYRIGHT

United States Copyright Office (www.copyright.gov)

The United States Copyright Office has a database of registered and renewed works created after 1978.

Catalog of Copyright Entries (http://archive.org/details/copyrightrecords)

Useful for researching the rights holder for an item created prior to 1978. Currently the Internet Archive has volumes going back to 1891.

ASCAP and BMI (https://www.ascap.com/Home/ace-title-search/index.aspx) and (http://repertoire.bmi.com/artistSearch.asp)

These two organizations are related to composers and musicians. Both are collective licensing organizations where you can contact one or the other to seek permission— or a license—to use a musical score.

Recording Industry Association of America (www.riaa.com/) and Harry Fox Agency (https://www.harryfox.com)

The two organizations listed above can be helpful for locating the rights holders of a sound recording.

Copyright Clearance Center (www.copyright.com)

The Copyright Clearance Center is another collective licensing organization that works mainly with book and journal article content. If the copyright holder works with CCC it will be relatively easy to request a license to use the work.

Artists' Rights Society (www.arsny.com/) and Visual Artists and Galleries Association (http://vagarights.com)

These two organizations are the main collective licensing organizations for visual artists.

Well-Intentioned Practice for Putting Digitized Collections of Unpublished Materials
Online (www.oclc.org/content/dam/research/activities/rights/practice.pdf)
This guide provides helpful suggestions for determining the copyright for unpublished, archival materials.

BEST PRACTICES AND GUIDES

Association for Library Collections and Technical Services: Minimum Digitization
Capture Recommendations, 2013. (www.ala.org/alcts/resources/preserv/
minimum-digitization-capture-recommendations)
A good, basic guide for those considering a digitization project. Covers different
formats, scanning quality, metadata, storage, file-naming protocols.

Federal Agencies Digitization Guidelines Initiative (FADGI) (www.digitization
guidelines.gov)
Blogs, news, and resources make this site a great place to start for both guidelines
and information related to specific issues including equipment, preservation of
audio materials, and comparisons of file formats.

Library of Congress: Building Digital Collections: Technical Information about American Memory Collections. (http://lcweb2.loc.gov/ammem/techdocs/digcols.html)

Protocols for Native American Archival Materials. (www2.nau.edu/libnap-p/
protocols.html)
The *Protocols* were written for librarians and archivists and has information on
rights, culturally sensitive information, access and treatment of Native American
materials. This is a good resource for those with collections containing materials
relating to Native American peoples.

COLLECTIONS

"Selecting Materials for Digitization," North Carolina Digital Heritage Center.
(www.digitalnc.org/about/participate/select)
This website contains good advice on selecting materials for digitization and provides links to example collections.

STATEWIDE AND NATIONAL COLLECTIONS

State Digital Resources: Memory Projects, Online Encyclopedias, Historical & Cultural Materials Collections. (https://www.loc.gov/rr/program/bib/statememory)
A list of digital collections compiled by the Library of Congress. Contents are
arranged by state. A good resource for finding possible partners, finding example collections, or verifying the uniqueness of your own collection before starting a project.

Library of Congress National Digital Newspaper Program (NDNP). (www.loc.gov/ndnp)

This site provides a listing of organizations which have received awards as part of the NDNP. Many of these organization may offer support for public libraries. The site includes a link to Chronicling America, an extensive collection of digitized newspapers.

FUNDING

IMLS. (www.imls.gov)

A source for information on available grants for libraries and museums. Deadlines, detailed requirements for those seeking grants, and times for webinars are provided.

Grants to State Library Administrative Agencies. IMLS. (www.imls.gov/programs)

Provides information on the state administrative agencies that provide LSTA funding.

Foundation Center Directory.(http://foundationcenter.org/fin/index.html)

The Foundation Directory is a searchable database designed to help people find grants. A network of libraries around the county provides access to this database and to print resources.

PRESERVATION

Northeast Document Conservation Center (NDCC). (https://www.nedcc.org/free -resources/digital-preservation)

This NDCC site contains guides, policy templates, planning tools, questionnaires, and information on training resources for those involved in digital preservation.

Library of Congress Digital Preservation Resources. (www.digitalpreservation.gov/ about/resources.html)

Some sections of this site are no longer being maintained, but information on preservation is available at basic to advanced levels. A great source for guides, standards, best practices, and tools.

Tony Gill, Anne J. Gilliland, Maureen Whalen, and Mary S. Woodley, ed. Murtha Baca, *Introduction to Metadata*. Los Angeles: Getty Research Institute, 2008. www.getty.edu/research/publications/electronic_publications/intrometadata.

"An online publication devoted to metadata, its types and uses, and how it can improve access to digital resources."

National Information Standards Organization (U.S.), (2007). *A Framework of Guidance for Building Good Digital Collections: A NISO Recommended Practice*. Baltimore, MD: National Information Standards Organization, 2007. www.niso.org/ publications/rp/framework3.pdf.

This framework provides an overview for creating digital collections, identifies resources and practices, and encourages community participation in further development of best practices.

Anne R. Kenney, Oya Rieger, and Research Libraries Group, *Moving Theory into Practice: Digital Imaging for Libraries and Archives*. Mountain View, CA: Research Libraries Group tutorial, 2000. https://www.library.cornell.edu/preservation/tutorial.

"This tutorial offers base-level information on the use of digital imaging to convert and make accessible cultural heritage materials."

"Sustainability of Digital Formats," Library of Congress website. (www.digitalpreservation.gov/formats)

A growing compilation of information on digital content formats and a great resource for determining the best file format for your project.

Digital POWRR project. (http://digitalpowrr.niu.edu)

Preserving Digital Objects with Restricted Resources (POWRR) provides workshops, papers, recommendations, and links to other resources.

ABOUT THE AUTHOR
AND CONTRIBUTORS

SUSANNE CARO is the government document librarian at the University of Montana, Missoula. She has presented at library conferences regarding how to access digitized educational resources. Previously she was the state document librarian and coordinator at the New Mexico State Library where she planned and implemented the creation of a digital collection of *El Palacio* magazine, the oldest museum publication in the country, dating back to 1913.

SAM MEISTER is currently the preservation communities manager at the Educopia Institute. He was previously the digital archivist and assistant professor in the Maureen and Mike Mansfield Library at the University of Montana-Missoula. He is also currently an instructor in the Society of American Archivists' Digital Archives Specialist Certificate Program and an instructor in the Library of Congress's Digital Preservation Outreach and Education Program. He holds an M.L.I.S. degree from San Jose State University.

TAMMY RAVAS is associate professor and visual and performing arts librarian at the University of Montana, Missoula. In 2010 Ravas received her Level One certification in Copyright Management and Leadership from the (now defunct) Center for Intellectual Property at the University of Maryland. She has presented at library conferences and other workshops regarding copyright and higher education. Her current research interests are educating undergraduates in copyright issues.

WENDY WALKER received her M.L.I.S. degree from San Jose State University in 2007. She worked for four years as the digital collections and metadata services librarian at the Henderson District Public Libraries and is now the digital initiatives librarian at the University of Montana.

INDEX

A

ACC (Arizona Centennial Commission), 13
access
    digital preservation and, 133–134
    digitization considerations for, 137–138
    digitization to improve, x–xi, xii, 4
ACPL
    See Allen County Public Library
Adams, Sue, 101–102
African Americans, 79–80
"Agreement on Guidelines for Classroom
    Copying in Not-For-Profit Educational
    Institutions with Respect to Books and
    Periodicals" (U.S. Copyright Office), 31–32
ALA
    See American Library Association
Albuquerque Historical Society, 119
Albuquerque/Bernalillo County Library
    System, New Mexico, 119
Alger, Dale, 124–125
Allen County Community Album digital
    project, 30
Allen County Public Library (ACPL)
    crowdsourcing, 89–92
    donor agreement of, 29–30
    volunteers at, 63, 64–65
Allenstown Public Library, New Hampshire,
    103
Alliance Library System (ALS), 143–144
American Folklife Center, Library of Congress,
    57–58
American Library Association (ALA)
    segregation and, 79–80
    StoryCorps @ your library, 58

American University, 40–41
archival storage
    implementation of, 142
    overview of, 138
    by Quincy Public Library, 144
Arizona Centennial Commission
    (ACC), 13
Arizona Centennial Legacy Projects,
    13
Arizona Historical Advisory
    Commission, 13
Arquette, Janis, 16–17
Artists' Rights Society (ARS), 38
ASCAP, 38
ascension numbers, 16
Association for Information and
    Image Management, 60
Atlanta-Fulton Public Library
    System, Atlanta, Georgia, 103
audiovisual materials
    copyright for, 44
    Division of Preservation and
        Access, 102–103
Aufderheide, Pat, 34
Australian Museum, 62
authenticity, 135
author
    copyright protection, 26
    copyright registration, 26–27
    length of copyright, 30
    rights of, 27
    See also copyright owner
availability, 134

B

backups, 138

Bangor Public Library, Maine
    digitization of posters at, 18
    funding for library digitization project,
        106–109

Banning District Library, California
    end-user policy of, 42
    local history collection of, 80–83

Barn-Bash: Making Hay for the Library
    (fundraising event), 111

Bartlesville Public Library, Oklahoma, 79

Beckwith, Frank Asahel, 19–21

Bell, Bill, 80–83

Belle W. Baruch Foundation, 105

Beloit College, x

Bensenville Community Public Library, Illinois,
    16–17

Bernier, Theresa "Resse," 122

Bethlehem Public Library, Delmar, New York
    digitization of *The Spotlight*, 10–11
    digitization of yearbooks at, 8–9
    documents in New York Heritage Digital
        Collections, 57

Big Read event (National Endowment for the
    Arts), 126, 128–129

Billings Public Library, Montana, 4, 65

birth certificates, 69

Blackburn, Fred, 122

Blackman, Andrea, 58–59

BMI, 38

Board of Education, Brown v., 79

Boston Globe (newspaper), 88

Boyce-Ditto Public Library, Mineral Wells,
    Texas, 65

Bradley University, 143

Bree, Palin, 65, 133

A Brief History of Madison (Public Schools of
    Madison), 66

Brown, Ruth, 79

Brown v. Board of Education, 79

Brownie camera, 82

Buffalo and Erie County Public Library system,
    New York, 98–99

Butler, Dwayne, 32–33

C

California Audio Visual Preservation Project
    (CAVPP), 44

California Digital Newspaper Collection
    (CDNC), 86, 87

Cambridge Chronicle (newspaper), 89

Cambridge Public Library, Massachusetts,
    87–89

camera, 82

Canoe Journeys photograph collection, 7–8

Capitol Records, Inc. v. Thomas-Rasset, 27

Caplan, Priscilla, 134–136

cassettes, 12–13, 14

Catalog of Copyright Entries (U.S. Copyright
    Office), 31, 38

Celaya, Dolores, 13

Center for Bibliographical Studies and
    Research (CBSR), 85–86

Charles Overstreet collection, 6–7

Charley's Flora (Overstreet), 6

checksums, 135

Chelsea District Library, Michigan
    community help with metadata at, 76–78
    fundraising for newspaper collection,
        109–112
    obituary database, 15
    volunteers for digitization at, 62

Chelsea Standard (newspaper), 110–112

Chicago Tribune (newspaper), 123–124, 125

Christian, Kimberly, 83

Christopher, George, 44

Chronicling America project (Library of
    Congress)
    description of, 11–12
    grants for digitization of newspapers, 102
    work of, 59

Cleveland Public Library, 53–56

Clifton Park-Halfmoon Public Library, 57

CML (Columbus Metropolitan Library), 53–56

*Code of Best Practices in Fair Use for Academic
    and Research Libraries* (Association of
    Research Libraries), 34–35, 42

Cole Museum, Bangor, Maine, 109

collaboration
    for conglomerate digital collections, 56–57
    crowdsourcing, 85–89
    for digital preservation, 142
    for digital projects, 51–53, 71
    IMLS grants for, 98
    for newspaper digitization, 11–12

collection, 1–2
    See also digital collection

collection-specific support, 57–60

Collins, Susan, 106–107

Columbus Metropolitan Library (CML), 53–56

Columbus–Lowndes Public Library, Columbus,
    Mississippi, 65

co-marketing, 118, 125–126

community
    Allen County Public Library and, 89–92
    Chelsea Public Library's fundraising for
        newspaper collection, 109–112
    crowdsourcing, 85–89
    digitization expectations of, ix–x

digitization of photos for preserving
    community memories, 4–6
histories, compiling, 78–84
local foundations, funding from, 104
local history collection, as accurate
    reflection of, 78–83
metadata for local memories, 76–78
oral histories, digitization of, 12–14
photographic collections to honor/
    remember, 6–7
relationship with library, 75–76
synopsis of, 92–93
Conable, Anne, 99
conglomerate collections, 56–57
Consultative Committee for Space Data
    Systems, 136
CONTENTdm sites, 17–18
copyright
    complaint, 42
    definition of, 26
    newspaper digitization and, 11–12
Copyright Clearance Center, 38
copyright owner
    donations to be digitized, copyright
        ownership, 27–29
    permission from, for digitization project,
        37–39
    rights of, 27, 45–46
    San Francisco History Center's digital
        collection and, 43, 45
copyrighted materials, digitizing
    copyright complaint, 42
    copyright law, definition of, 26
    donations to be digitized, 27–29
    donor agreement, 29–30
    end-user policies, 41–42
    fair use, 31–35
    kinds of works protected by copyright, 26
    length of copyright, 30
    libraries and archives exception, 36–37
    orphan works, 39–41
    permission for copyrighted work, 37–39
    public domain, 30–31
    registration with USCO, 26–27
    right to, 25
    rights of copyright owners, 27
    San Francisco Public Library case study,
        42–45
    synopsis of, 45–46
Cory, Dona, 6–7
cost, of digital preservation, 141
"Creating Digital Collections of Archival and
    Special Collections Materials" principle,
    34–35
Crews, Kenneth, 32–33, 46

Cronin, Mary
    call for donations, 70
    on digital collection, xi
    on funding, 104
    work with volunteers, 67–68, 69
crowdsourcing
    at Allen County Public Library, 89–92
    benefits of, 87–88
    for connecting people and history, 89
    description of, 85
    motivation of crowd, 86–87
    newspaper searchability improvements
        with, 88–89
    software for, 85–86
    synopsis of, 92
    trust in crowd, 86
cultural diversity
    local history collection, as accurate
        reflection of, 78–83
    neglected history, organized effort to
        collect, 83–84
Cummings, E. E., 66

D
Daigle, Barbara, 107–109
Daigle, Eugene, 107–109
Daigle, James, 108
Daniel E. Koshland San Francisco History
    Center, 42–45
"A Day in Allen County" photography contest, 91
deed of gift, 29–30
Delta City Library, Utah, 18–21
digital collection
    case study in Delta City, Utah, 18–21
    choice of materials to digitize, 3–14
    choice of, questions for, 22
    collaboration/partnerships for, 51–53
    digitization process, questions for, 1–2
    hosting, 56–57
    intention of, 2–3
    organization/description of, 14–18
    size of materials, 18
    synopsis of, 21–22
    See also marketing
Digital Dissemination of Archival Collections
    grant, 103
Digital Imaging Grant Program, 103
digital inclusion, x
Digital Inclusion Survey, x
digital objects
    digital preservation goals, 133–136
    inventory of, 142
digital preservation
    considerations beyond technology, 140–141
    general concepts of, 133–136

digital preservation (*cont'd*)
    options/tools for, 140
    Quincy Public Library case study, 142–145
    standards, 136–137
    steps for action, 141–142
    strategies for, 137–139
    synopsis of, 145
Digital Preservation Management Tutorial, 140
digitization
    for access improvement, x–xi
    at Allen County Public Library, 89–92
    choice of materials to digitize, 3–14
    community expectations for, ix–x
    cost of, 53, 141
    digital preservation strategies, 137–138
    federal grants for, 97–103
    as first act of digital preservation, 133
    of newspapers at Chelsea Public Library,
      109–112
    of photos for local history collection, 81–83
    as preservation tool, xi–xii
    process, questions for, 1–2
    supporting regional libraries for, 53–56
    vendor, working with, 60–62
    volunteers, case study, 66–70
    volunteers for, 62–66
    See also copyrighted materials, digitizing
digitization hubs, 53–56
Digitization Projects Registry, 12
Dillon, Dennis, 117
discrimination, 79–80
Division of Preservation and Access, 102–103
Documentary Filmmakers Statement of Best
    Practices in Fair Use (Aufderheide & Jaszi), 34
donations
    to Chelsea Public Library, 111–112
    copyright issues of, 25
    copyright ownership, digitization and,
      27–29
    of documents to Madison Public Library, 70
donor agreement
    for copyright, 29–30
    overview of, 29–30
    summary of, 46
Dover Public Library, New Hampshire, 9–10
Drouin, Jeremy, 61
Dublin Core schema, 17–18

E

Early Heroes and Heroines of Illinois History:
    An Interactive Multimedia Memory Montage
    collection, 143
Early Illinois Women and Other Unsung
    Heroes website, 143
Eaton, New Hampshire, 66

e-books, ix
Elgin Image award, 126
emulation
    description of, 139
    for renderability, 136
    for retrieval of images, 144
end-user policies, 41–42

F

Facebook
    Gail Borden Public Library's marketing
      with, 128
    for marketing of digital collection,
      119–120
    Oak Park Public Library on, 125
    percentage of people using, 119
    Seattle Public Library and, 121
fair use
    best practices codes, 34–35
    Fair Use Checklist, 32–33
    orphan works and, 40
    overview of, 31–32
    summary of, 46
Fair Use Checklist (Crews & Butler), 32–33, 46
Fairmont Public Library, Fairmont, Nebraska,
    52–53
Family History Index, 15
family photographs, 5
Federal Communications Commission, x
federal grants
    grant proposal for Oregon City Library,
      101–102
    Institute of Museum and Library Services,
      98–100
    LSTA grants, 100–101
    National American Library Services:
      Enhancement Grants, 100
    National Endowment for the Humanities,
      102–103
    National Historical Publications and
      Records Commission, 103
    overview of, 97–98
    synopsis of, 112–113
file formats
    preservation planning and, 139
    selection of for digitization, 137
film, rights status of, 44
fixity, 135, 138
Flickr, 86–87
FlipBook software, 144
Flood 1010 NS StoryCorps @ Your Library
    projects, 58–59
Flora Public Library, Missouri
    Charles Overstreet collection, 6–7
    end-user policy of, 41–42

Foundation Center Directory, 106, 113
foundations
    finding, 106
    funding from, 104–106
    grants from, 113
Frank Beckwith Collection, 19–21
Frazier, Allen, 7–8
Friends of the Library foundations, 106
funding
    for digital projects, 52
    federal grants, 97–103
    from foundations, 104–106
    fundraising by Chelsea Public Library,
        109–112
    from individuals/gifts, 106–109
    state grants, 103–104
    synopsis of, 112–113
fundraising
    for newspaper collection, case study,
        109–112
    synopsis of, 113

G
Gadsden Public Library, Alabama
    outsourcing of digitization projects, 61–62
    photograph collection of Bobby Scarboro,
        16, 18
Gail Borden Public Library, Elgin, Illinois,
    126–129
Galway Central School Collaborative, 57
Galway Public Library, 56–57
Gaylord and Dorothy Donnelley Foundation,
    104–105
Geiger, Brian, 85–86
George Blood Audio/Video, 14
"Georgetown County Hurricane Collection"
    (Georgetown County Library), 5
Georgetown County Library, South Carolina
    digitization of photos at, 5–6
    end-user policy of, 41
    grant for, 104–105
    online images, use of, xi
Gerding, Stephanie, 106
Ghoshal, Sumantra, 87
Giant Trees of California (film), 44
gifts, 106–109
Goode, Richard, 58
Google News Archive, 12
grants
    for Chelsea Public Library, 109–110
    federal, 97–103
    for library digital project, 52, 53
    for Oak Park Public Library, 125
    state, 103–104
    synopsis of, 112–113

Grants to State Library Administrative
    Agencies, 100–101
grants.gov, 104
Great Basin Museum, Utah, 18
Great Recession, 75
Greathouse, Deborah B., 19–21
"Guidelines with Respect to Music" (U.S.
    Copyright Office?), 31–32
Gunnison, John Williams, 18

H
Hacking Hemingway: Cracking the Code to the
    Vault project, 125–126
Hagenhofer, Faith, 7–8
handling, 4
hardware, 134, 135–136
Harry Fox Agency, 38
HCNC (Historic Cambridge Newspaper
    Collection), 88–89
Heritage, 110
Hernando County Public Library, Brooksville,
    Florida, 121–122
Highland Park Public Library, Illinois, 123–124
Hispanic Heritage Month Celebration, 129
Historic Albuquerque Inc., 119
Historic Cambridge Newspaper Collection
    (HCNC), 88–89
historical societies, 119
history
    accurate reflection of community, 78–83
    crowdsourcing for connecting people to, 89
    librarian's role in compiling/preserving
        local histories, 78
    neglected history, organized effort to
        collect, 83–85
    See also oral histories
hosting
    for digital newspaper collection, 59
    of library digital collection, 17–18, 56–57
House of Seven Generations collection, 100
Houston Metropolitan Research Center of the
    Houston Public Library, 13–14
Houston Oral History Project, 13–14
Houston Public Library, Texas, 13–14
Humanities Collections and Reference
    Resources grant, 102
Huntley Area Public Library District, Huntley,
    Illinois, 103

I
identity, of digital objects, 134
Illinois Alive; The Heritage and Texture of
    a Pivotal State during the First Century of
    Statehood collection, 143
Illinois Digital Archive, 103, 145

Illinois Digital Platform, 123
Illinois State Library, 103, 144
Illinois State Talking Book and Braille Service, 143
IMLS
    See Institute of Museum and Library Services
index, 17
index cards, 15
individuals, funding from, 106–109
information package, 136–137
Instagram, 119–120, 121
Institute of Museum and Library Services (IMLS)
    on cooperative digital projects, 52
    grant information on website of, 104
    grants from, 97–100, 112
    on increase in library visits, 75
    LSTA grants from, 100–101
    Native American Library Services: Enhancement Grants, 100
    on number of e-books in libraries, ix
    on use of volunteers, 62
International Federation of Library Associations and Institutions, 126, 127
Internet
    digitizing to improve access, x–xi
    number of people with Internet access, x
Internet Archive
    CAVPP, 44
    for newspaper digitization project, 12
    Wayback Machine, 144
interviews
    collection-specific support, 57–58
    copyright ownership for, 28
inventory, of digital content, 142
Ireland, Kitty, 120–121

J
Jamestown S'Klallam Tribal Library, Sequim, Washington, 100
Jaszi, Peter, 34
Jefferson Parish Library, 12
Jenkins, Leanne, 100
Johnson, Patricia, 51
Jones, Harold A., 15

K
Kaminski House Museum, 105
Kansas City Public Library, Missouri, 61
Kirkpatrick, Geoff
    on digitization of *The Spotlight*, 10–11
    digitization of yearbooks by, 8–9
Kitchener, Amy, 84
Kodak, 82
Krahmer, Ana, 61, 105–106

L
Lane, Melissa G., 75, 127–128
Lemonius, Roland, 14
libraries and archives exception, 36–37
library
    collaboration/partnerships for digital projects, 51–53
    community's relationship with, 75–76
    digitization, reasons for, ix–xii
    local history, need to collect/preserve, 78–85
Library Bill of Rights (American Library Association), 79
Library Journal, 79, 109
library newsletter, 67
Library of Congress
    American Folklife Center, 57–58
    American Folkways Center Veterans History Project, 70
    Chronicling America project, 11–12, 59
    on copyright, 25
    for digital collections initiatives, 57
    end-user policies resources, 41
    Flickr crowdsourcing project, 86–87
    support for oral history collection, 58
library patrons, ix–x
Library Services Act, 100–101
Library Services and Technology Act (LSTA)
    grant for Quincy Public Library, 145
    grants from, 100–101, 112
library staffing
    See staffing
Lipscomb University, 58
local foundations, funding from, 104
local history
    accurate reflection of community, 78–83
    Chelsea Public Library's fundraising for newspaper collection, 109–112
    need to collect/preserve, 78
    neglected history, organized effort to collect, 83–85
Local History Live! YouTube channel, 121–122
Los Angeles Public Library, California, 83–84

M
MacKellar, Pam, 106
Madison, New Hampshire, 65–66
Madison Public Library, New Hampshire
    funding from local foundations for, 104
    survey on community ranking of library, xi
    volunteers case study, 66–70
Maney, Jen, 13
Marget, Wanda, 52–53, 97
marketing
    case study, Gail Borden Public Library, 126–129

co-marketing, 125–126
definition of, 117–118
of Frank Beckwith Collection, 20
public relations marketing, 122–125
synopsis of, 129–130
types of, 118
word of mouth/social media, 118–122
Marshall Cavendish Award for Excellence in
Library Programming, 126
materials
choosing digital collection, 3–14
size of, digitization choice and, 18
Maxwell, Alexander, 78
McDade, Barbara, 106–109
McGarrity, Brittany, 122
McKune, Catherine, 109
McQuown, Shan, 122
media outlets, 122–125
Meloche, Emily
Chelsea Public Library's fundraising for
newspaper collection, 109–112
community help with metadata, 76–78
Memorandum of Understanding (MOU),
55–56
Menchaca, Martha, 80
Merriam-Webster Dictionary, 118
Merritt, LeRoy Charles, 79
metadata
for collections that are already organized/
described, 16
community involvement in creating, 76–78
considerations about, 2
crowdsourcing and, 87
for digital collection, choices for, 14–15
digitization decisions about, 137–138
entry by volunteers at Madison Public
Library, 68, 69
for historical photographs, 7
for library digital project, 52
outsourcing digitization and, 2
recognition of people in, 68, 70
vendor scanning and, 61
by volunteers at Madison Public Library,
66–67
volunteers for, 62, 63–65
Metadata Encoding & Transmission Standard
(METS), 15
microfilm
degradation of, 10
digitization of, 109–112
Mid-Illinois Talking Book Center, 143
migration
description of, 139
for renderability, 136
Millary County Chronicle (newspaper), 19, 20–21
Mindset List, x

money
  See funding
Montana Memory Project, 4, 125
Montono, Oscar, 13
Moose License Plate Conservation Grants, 103
More Charley's Flora (Overstreet), 6
Moretta, Christina, 43–45
Morgan, W. D., 5
MOU (Memorandum of Understanding), 55–56
Mukurtu (content management system), 83
music performances, 28–29
musical works, 38
Musselshell Historical Museum, Roundup,
Montana, 124

N
Nafe, Emilia, 123–124
Nahapiet, Janine, 87
NASA, 86, 87
Nashville Public Library, 58–59
National Digital Newspaper Project (NDNP)
Chronicling America project, 12
funding for newspaper digitization, 106
grants from, 102
vendor digitization and, 61
work of, 59–60
National Endowment for the Arts, 126, 128–129
National Endowment for the Humanities
(NEH)
Chronicling America project, 12, 59
grant information on website of, 104
grants from, 99, 102–103, 112
National Historical Publications and Records
Commission, 103, 112
National Leadership Grants for Libraries,
97–98
National Library, Finland, 86
National Medal for Museum and Library
Service, 126
Native American Library Services:
Enhancement Grants, 100
Native Americans, 82–83
NDNP
  See National Digital Newspaper Project
Nebraska Library Commission, 52–53
NEH
  See National Endowment for the
  Humanities
Nelson, Iris, 143, 144
New Hampshire, 103
New York Heritage Digital Collections, 56–57
New York Public Library
crowdsourcing used by, 88
diverse population/collection of, 78
New York Times (newspaper), 88
newsletter, 128

newspapers
  Chelsea Public Library's fundraising for,
    109–112
  crowdsourcing for improving searchability
    of, 88–89
  crowdsourcing to correct text in digitized,
    85–86
  digitization of, 10–11
  digitization of at Allen County Public
    Library, 90
  digitization of, support for, 59–60
  in Frank Beckwith Collection, 19–20
  funding for digitization, 105–106
  grant proposal for digitization at Oregon
    City Library, 101–102
  grants for digitization of, 102
  marketing of digital collection with,
    123–124
  Millary County Chronicle, digitization of,
    19–20
  partnerships for preservation of, 11–12
  scanning options for, 18
Nicholas County Public Library, Kentucky, 10
Nickerson, Lucy, 70
Nisqually Tribal Library, Olympia, Washington,
  7–8
Nov, Oded, 86
NY 3Rs Association, 57

O
Oak Park Public Library, Illinois, 103, 125–126
Oasis Albuquerque, 119
obituary database, 15
Obituary File, 15
O'Brien, Tim, 128, 129
OCLC, 75
O'Connell, Eileen, ix, 119
OCR character correction, 85–86, 88–89
Ohio Public Library Information Network, 53
Oklahoma Correctional Industries, 9–10
Oneal, Angela, 54–56
Open Archival Information System (OAIS),
  136–138
oral histories
  collection-specific support, 57–58
  copyright ownership for, 28
  digitization of, 12–13
  neglected history, organized effort to
    collect, 83–84
  preservation of, 13–14
  project of Madison Public Library, 70
  YouTube marketing and, 121–122
Oregon City Library, 101–102
Oregon Digital Newspaper Program, 101–102

organization
  of digital collection, 14–18
  subject-based organization, 16–18
orphan works, 39–41, 46
Orphan Works: Statement of Best Practices
  (Society of American Archivists), 40
outreach
  benefits of, 92
  importance of, 92
  marketing *vs.*, 118
  See also community; marketing
outsourcing
  of digital preservation, 140
  of digitization projects, 71
  to digitization vendor, 2
  vendors, working with, 60–62
Overstreet, Charles, 6–7, 78

P
partnerships
  for digital preservation, 142
  for digital projects, 51–53
  for funding for newspaper digitization,
    105–106
  of Gail Borden Public Library, for
    marketing, 127–129
  for newspaper digitization project, 59–60
  for oral history collections, 57–59
  for scanning, 53–56
patrons, library, ix–x
Pennsylvania State University Libraries, 106
permission, for copyrighted work, 37–39
Pew Research Center
  Digital Inclusion Survey, x
  on Facebook use, 119
  on Internet use for government research, xi
Photo Friends of the L.A. Public Library, 84
photographs
  Allen County Public Library's request for, 91
  copyright ownership for, 28
  current images/cultural expression, 7–8
  digital collection, choosing, 3
  digital collections to honor/remember, 6–7
  digital images to reduce handling, improve
    access, 4
  digitization for preservation of, xi
  digitization for preserving community
    memories, 4–6
  in Frank Beckwith Collection, 19–20
  for local history collection, 79–83
  neglected history, organized effort to
    collect, 83–84
  for social media marketing, 120–121
  subject-based organization for, 16–18

yearbooks, 8–9
yearbooks, free scanning of, 9–10
Pima County Public Library, Arizona, 13
Pinterest, 121
planning, preservation, 139
poetry contest, 91
policy, digital preservation, 140–141
Portal to Texas History, 105–106
posters
    at Bangor Public Library, 18, 106–109
    for marketing of digital collection, 119
preservation
    digitization as tool for, xi–xii
    digitization of photos for preserving
        community memories, 4–6
    "libraries and archives exception" for, 36
    of local history, 78–85
    of oral histories, 12–14
    planning, 139
    See also digital preservation
press releases
    for newspapers, 123, 124
    for radio, 125
    overview of, 122–123
public domain, 30–31, 43
Public Library of Cincinnati and Hamilton
    County, 53–56
public relations marketing
    by Gail Borden Public Library, 127–128
    marketing of digital collection with, 118
    newspapers, 123–124
    press releases, 122
    radio, 124–125
Public Relations Society of America, 122
public service announcements (PSAs), 122, 124

Q
Quincy Area Historic Photo Collection, 145
Quincy Public Library, 142–145

R
radio, 124–125
Ranlett, L. Felix, 107
rare materials, digitization of, 1–2
RDA, 15
Reaching Across Illinois Library System
    (RAILS), 144
Recording Industry Association of America, 38
Reflections: Flowing through Time event, 128
Reflections of Galway (Galway Public Library &
    Galway Central School Collaborative), 57
registration
    of copyright, 45
    with USCO, 26–27

renderability, of digital objects, 135–136
rights, of copyright owners, 27
Robins, Kathy, 4
Roosevelt, Franklin D., 44
Roundup Community Library, 124–125
Rumery, Dean, 107
Rumery, Joyce, 106–109

S
San Francisco Public Library (SFPL), 42–45
Santa Paula, California, 80
Sausalito News (newspaper), 86
scanning
    cost of, 53
    of newspapers, 10–11
    partnerships for, 52
    of photos for local history collection, 82
    size of materials and, 18
    supporting regional libraries, 53–56
    by vendor, 60–62
    by volunteers, 63–65
    by volunteers at Madison Public Library,
        66–67
    yearbooks, free scanning of, 9–10
Scarboro, Bobby, 16, 18
Scott, Craig
    digitization for preservation, 78
    outsourcing of digitization projects, 61–62
    photograph collection and, 16
scrapbooks, 19–20
Seattle Public Library, 120–121
segregation, 79–80
seniors, 76–78
17 U.S.C. Sec. 108, 36–37
SFPL (San Francisco Public Library), 42–45
Shades of LA collection, Los Angeles Public
    Library, 83–84
Sharp, Fawn, 8
size
    of materials to be digitized, 18
    outsourcing of digitization projects and, 61
SLAA (State Library Administrative Agency),
    52, 100–101
Slossar, Bobbi, 69
Smithsonian Institute
    crowdsourcing used by, 86
    Digital Volunteers Transcription Center,
        87–88
Snyder, Nicole, 89
social media
    Gail Borden Public Library, marketing case
        study, 126–127
    marketing of digital collection with, 118–122
    Oak Park Public Library on Facebook, 125

Society of American Archivists, 40
software
    for crowdsourcing, 85–86
    for digital preservation, 140
    digital preservation and, 134, 135–136
    Quincy Public Library and, 144
Somers, Frank, 1, 10–11
Soundsafe Archive, 14
The Spotlight (newspaper), 10–11
staffing
    collaborations/partnerships for digital
        projects, 51–53
    collection-specific support, 57–60
    digitization support, 53–56
    hosting digital collection, 56–57
    Madison Public Library, volunteers case
        study, 66–70
    synopsis of, 71
    vendor, working with, 60–62
    volunteers, 62–66
standards
    for digital preservation, 136–137
    for metadata, 15
*State Digital Resources: Memory Projects, Online
    Encyclopedias, Historical & Cultural Materials
    Collections* (Library of Congress), 57
state grants
    overview of, 103–104
    synopsis of, 112–113
state libraries
    cooperative digital projects, 52
    partnership with for digital preservation, 142
State Library Administrative Agency (SLAA),
    52, 100–101
*Statement of Best Practices in Fair Use of
    Collections Containing Orphan Works for
    Libraries, Archives, and Other Memory
    Institutions* (UC Berkeley & American
    University), 40–41, 42
storage, 18
    See also archival storage
StoryCorps, 57–59
StoryTubes: Kids Go Live with Books program,
    126, 127
*Strategic Marketing in Library and Information
    Science* (Dillon), 117
students, 65, 90–92
subject-based organization, 16–18
Sustainable Heritage Network, 83

T
technology
    digital preservation and, 133–134
    preservation planning and, 139

TexShare, 101
TexTreasures grant, 101
The Things They Carried (O'Brien), 128, 129
Thomas-Rasset, Capitol Records, Inc. v., 27
"three-legged stool" analogy, 140
Tocker Foundation, 105–106
Toledo-Lucas County Public Library, 53–56
Topaz Museum, Utah, 18
town columns, 69
town reports, 69
training
    of volunteers, 63, 71
    of volunteers at Madison Public Library,
        67–68
transcription, 85–89
Tremblay, Carolyn, 9–10, 78
Trotter, Greg, 124
trust, 86
Twitter, 119–120, 121

U
understandability, of digital objects, 134–135
United States Newspaper Project, 59
University of California Berkeley, 40–41, 44
University of Maine Library, 108
University of North Texas (UNT) Libraries,
    105–106
University of Oregon, 101–102
University of Utah, 19
unpublished works, 37
U.S. Census, x
U.S. Constitution, 26
U.S. Copyright Office (USCO)
    Catalog of Copyright Entries, 31, 38
    orphan works and, 39–40
    registration of work with, 26–27
U.S. Supreme Court, 79–80
Utah State Library, 19

V
VAGA (Visual Artists and Galleries Association), 38
Vance-Ali, Mona
    preservation of original materials, 78
    on volunteers, 65, 66
vendor
    crowdsourcing software, 85–86
    outsourcing to, 2
    working with, 60–62
Veridian, 85, 88
Veterans History Project, 58–59, 70
viability, of digital objects, 135
videos
    copyright ownership for, 29
    YouTube, marketing with, 121–122

Viglucci, Christina, 129
Visual Artists and Galleries Association (VAGA), 38
Visual Resources Association Core (VRA), 15
vital records, 69
volunteer coordinator, 63
volunteers
    at Allen County Public Library, 89–92
    community involvement encouraged by, 76
    for digital projects, 71
    for digitization projects, 62
    Donald Weber, 64–65
    drawbacks of, 65–66
    for Los Angeles Public Library's Shades of LA project, 84
    Madison Public Library case study, 66–70
    metadata help from community, 76–78
    strategies for successful, 63
    students, 65
VRA (Visual Resources Association Core), 15

W
Warren, Julie, xi, 5–6
Washington Rural Heritage Project (WRHP), 7–8
Weber, Donald, 64–65
website
    hosted site for digital collection, 17–18
    by Quincy Public Library, 142–145
Wedell, Sara, 112
Wikipedia, 86
Winning Grants: A How-to-Do-It Manual for Librarians with Multimedia Tutorials and Grant Development Tools (Gerding & MacKellar), 106

Witcher, Curt
    on community engagement at library, 91–92
    on donor agreement, 29–30
    volunteer, working with, 64–65
Wood, John, 142
word of mouth
    marketing by Gail Borden Public Library, 127–128
    marketing of digital collection with, 118–120
    social media marketing, 120–122
works
    copyright, types of works protected by, 26
    registration with USCO, 26–27
World War II
    photos in Charles Overstreet collection, 6, 7
    posters at Bangor Public Library, 18, 106–109
    StoryCorps stories from veterans, 59

Y
yearbooks
    choice of for digital collection, 8–9
    free scanning of, 9–10
YouTube
    for marketing of digital collection, 119–120, 121–122
    StoryTubes: Kids Go Live with Books program, 127

Z
Zarndt, Frederick, 86